PAPIER MÂCHÉ
DYEING &
LEATHERWORK

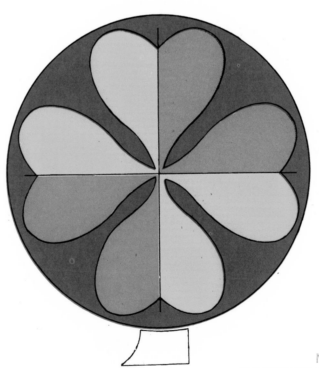

Franklin Watts, Inc
845 Third Avenue
New York, N.Y. 10022

First published 1972
© 1972 Santillana, S. A. de Ediciones

First English edition 1973
English translation © 1973 Macdonald
and Company (Publishers) Limited.
49/50 Poland Street, London W1A 2LG
Translated by Nicholas Fry
First American publication 1973 by Franklin Watts, Inc.

Printed in Spain - Impreso en España
Gráficas VELASCO, S. A.
Antonio de Cabezón, 13 - Madrid-34

Library of Congress Catalog Card Number: 73-2303

SBN 531-02632-9
Depósito legal: M. 13.397-1973

Papier Mâché, Dyeing and Leatherwork

The projects in this book are divided into five grades, from very simple to advanced. The color key below shows the grades and corresponding symbols, which are repeated at the beginning of each project for easy reference. The very simple projects are designed for younger children but the grades are only intended as a rough guide. Very young children may need some help.

 Very simple

 Easy

 Moderately easy

 More complex

 Advanced

Papier Mâché, Dyeing and Leatherwork is the seventh book in the *Color Crafts* series. Each of the sections opens with a number of colored pages where the basic techniques are explained.

The first tasks in each section are more suitable for beginners, while those toward the end of each section call for more skill and will be suitable for those who have already had some practice with the techniques and tools.

In the first few projects of the leather section, only this material is used. Further on, leather is combined with other materials such as metal wire, imitation jewels, etc.

The section on dyeing is divided into two parts. The first deals with the use of commercial hot dyes on materials tied and knotted to produce different patterns. This process is known as "shiboris," which is Japanese for "knot," since this technique of tie-dyeing apparently comes from Japan. The second part of the section has examples of "batik," a technique of Malayan origin which involves covering the parts of the cloth which are to be kept free of dye with wax and then dipping the work in one or more baths of cold dye.

The dyeing work involves more complex techniques and is more suitable for older children, although smaller children could attempt these projects under the close supervision of an adult.

The third section of the book deals with objects made of papier mâché. Three different methods are used here: paper which is soaked in PVA glue or cellulose paste and then folded into the shape of an object; paper pulp which is modeled into shape; and paper pulp which is applied over a framework of cardboard, wood or wire. Once you have mastered the techniques you can try creating objects which are all your own, from the design to the final decoration.

In many projects, we recommend the use of PVA glue, an all-purpose white opaque glue which can be used in the following ways: (1) undiluted as a simple adhesive or glue; (2) diluted to make papier mâché; (3) as a varnish or top coat; (4) mixed with paint to give a shiny finish. Cellulose wallpaper paste can also be used for making papier mâché. We do not recommend flour and water paste as this tends to smell after a while.

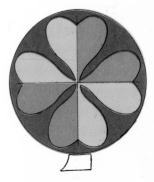

Working with leather

Leather is a material which is pleasant, clean and easy to use. It can be obtained in a wide variety of colors, and it is not difficult to dye raw leather, since it takes any of the dyes used for cloth very well.

Three different types of leather are used for the projects in this book: hard leather, soft leather and morocco.

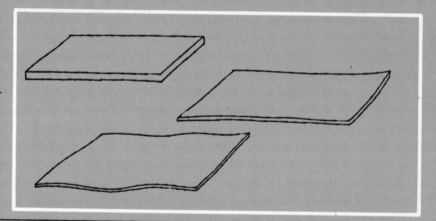

Hard leather can only be cut with a knife. Always use a scalpel-type knife, with a handle, such as draftsmen use for cutting cardboard. It is easier to use and safer than any other type of knife.

Soft leather and morocco can be cut with scissors, almost as easily as a thickish piece of cloth.

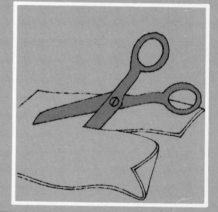

In order to sew hard leather, first you need to punch holes for the stitches with a punch or bradawl. Soft leather and morocco, on the other hand, can easily be sewn with a needle threaded with linen thread or a thin strip of leather.

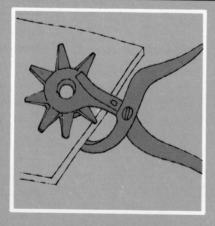

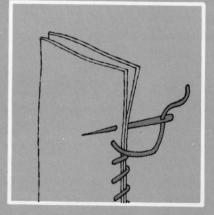

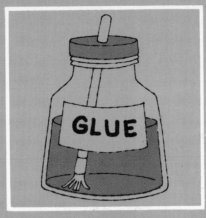

Both hard leather, soft leather and morocco are best stuck with a type of glue known as PVA, which can be obtained in any good hardware shop.

This glue is of the type known as contact adhesive, and the method of using it is to coat thoroughly both of the parts to be stuck down and leave them to dry for a few minutes, then press the two surfaces firmly together.

Leave them for a while under a weight until the glue is completely dry and the two pieces are firmly stuck together.

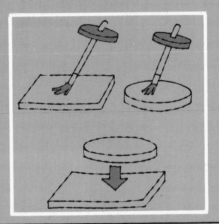

The most common tools used in leatherwork are a bradawl, a punch and a riveting tool.

The bradawl is a thick metal needle mounted in a wooden or plastic handle, and is used for piercing holes in thick leather. The punch is a pincer-like tool which can cut out round pieces of leather of different sizes.

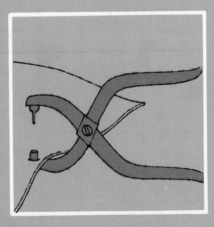

To use the riveting tool, place the rivets in holes previously made with the punch. You should practice using rivets before trying to include them in a particular piece of work; a certain amount of physical strength is needed to mount the rivet firmly in place. Very young children should be helped by an older person.

MATERIALS:

- ● Pieces of soft leather in different colors
- ● Piece of cardboard $8\frac{1}{2} \times 6\frac{1}{2}$ in.
- ● Scissors
- ● PVA glue
- ● Strips of morocco 1 in. wide to make the frame

MOSAIC

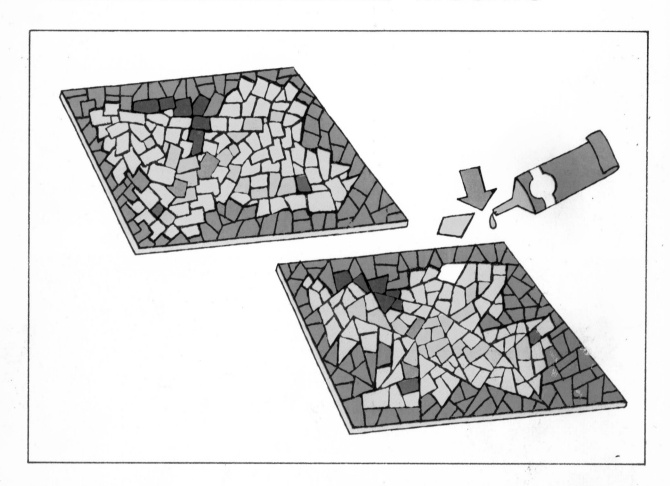

Draw a design for the mosaic on a piece of paper. Cut up the design into pieces and use these pieces as patterns to cut up the leather.

Place the pieces of leather on the cardboard to make up the design. When they are all in place, stick them down.

Then leave the work pressed under some books for a few hours until the glue is completely dry.

Now make the frame. Glue the back of the strips of red morocco and wrap them around the edge of the cardboard so that half the strip comes over the front of the mosaic and the other half is stuck to the back.

Press the mosaic under some books again until the glue is completely dry.

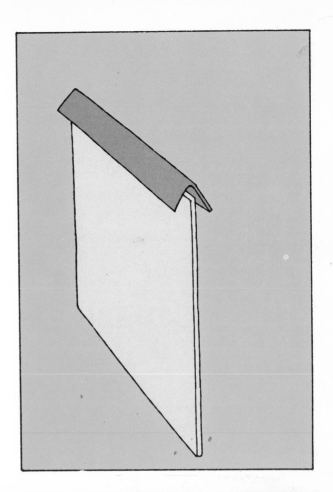

JIGSAW PUZZLE

Draw the picture for the jigsaw puzzle on the cardboard. Cut the drawing into a lot of different shapes.

Cut a piece of morocco to fit each piece of cardboard. Stick the pieces of leather to the pieces of cardboard.

Now make the frame. Stick strips of dark morocco ¼ in. wide to strips of cardboard of the same size. Stick these to the edges of the plywood which forms the base of the jigsaw.

Now you can put all the jigsaw pieces together to make the picture, inside the frame.

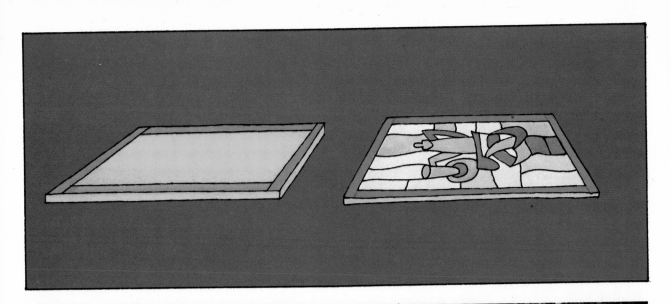

BOOK MARK

Cut the strip of leather using the shape shown in the drawing as a guide. Then make cuts about 2 in. deep for the fringes.

Draw the different parts of the flower on the pieces of colored leather. Cut them out with a very sharp pointed pair of scissors.

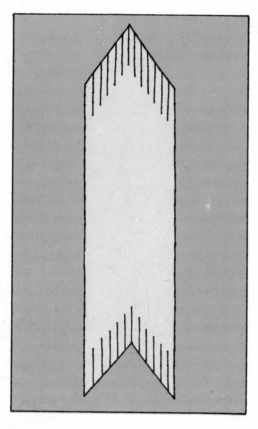

Stick these into the strip of leather. Take care that the glue does not stain the leather of the background if it is a pale color.

Press the book mark under some books for an hour or two before using it.

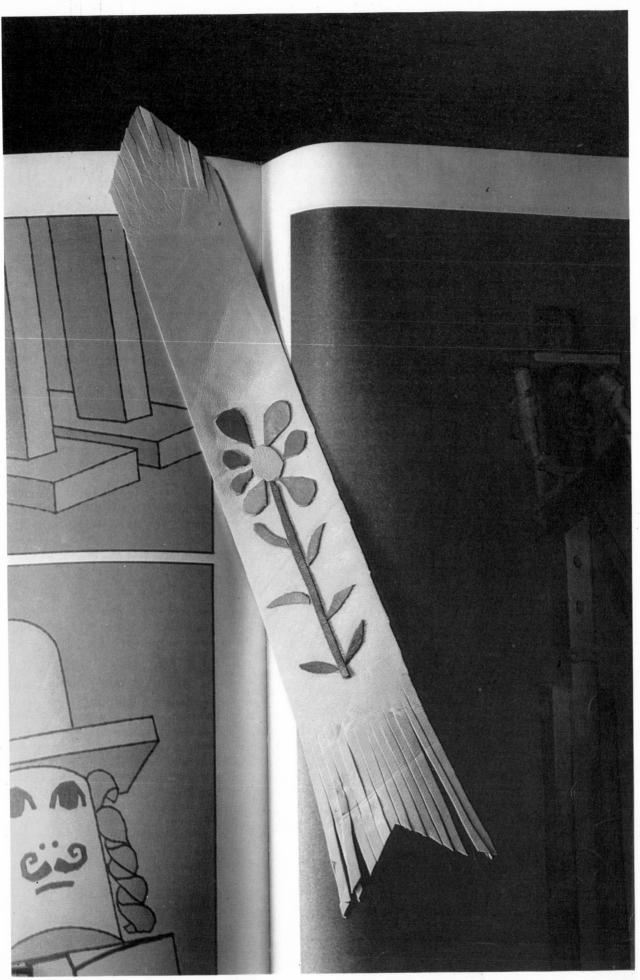

BAG FOR MARBLES

Punch 24 holes in the round piece of leather as shown in the drawing. They should be about 1 in. apart.

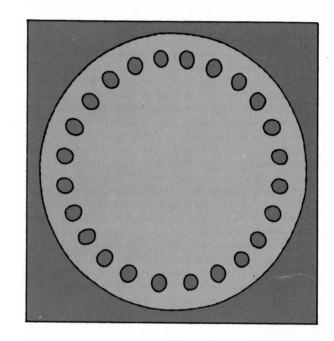

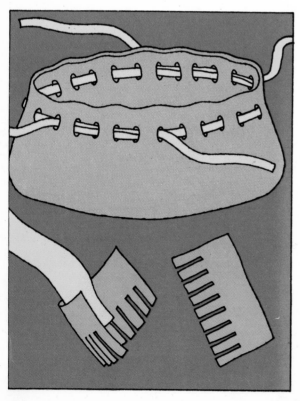

Pass the long strips of leather through the holes as shown in the drawing.

To make the tassels on the ends of these strips, cut fringes along one side of the rectangles of leather. Put a small amount of glue on the part above the fringes, and roll them around the ends of the strips.

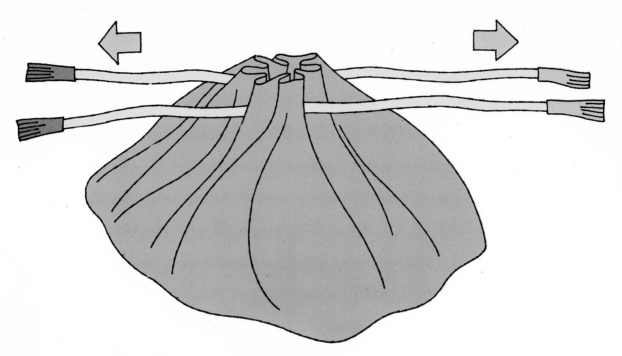

This bag will hold up to 30 marbles. To close it, pull the ends of the leather strips.

FLOWERPOT MAT

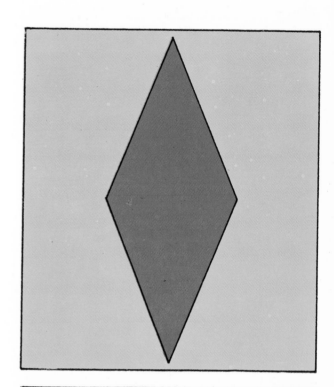

Arrange the diamond-shaped pieces of leather in a star and stick them down on the piece of plastic. When they are all glued in place, put the star under a pile of books while the glue dries.

Then cut the plastic flush with the edge of the leather so that it cannot be seen. The plastic prevents water from the flower pot from harming the table.

18

FLOWERS

Cut the different pieces of the daisy from leather of different colors, as shown in the drawing.

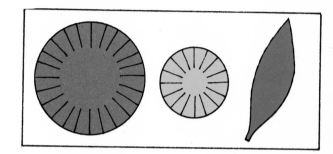

Place the two parts of the flower on top of one another and sew on a button so that the stitches pass right through them, holding the flower together.

Stitch a piece of hard leather cord to the back of the flower to form the stem. Fasten the leaves to the stem with a drop of glue.

To make the primrose, use exactly the same method as for the previous flower, and follow the drawing (bottom right).

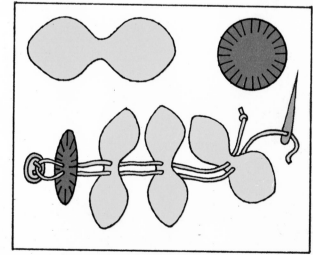

21

MATERIALS:

- Piece of hard leather 8×4 in.
- Round piece of the same leather 2½ in. in diameter
- Strong thread
- Punch and knife

DICE BOX

Use the punch to make the holes for the decoration and the seams in both pieces of leather (see drawing, top right). Embroider the sides, using the holes made with the punch.

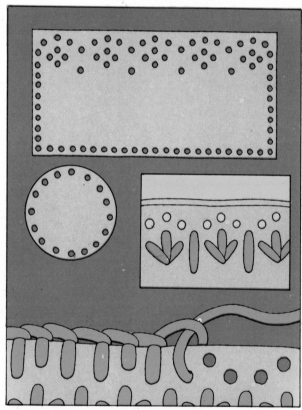

There are two different ways of passing the thread through the holes: one is to thread it on a thick needle or bodkin; the other is to dip the end in hot wax. When the wax begins to cool, twist the end of the cotton into a point and leave it to harden.

The waxed tip of the thread can then be easily pushed through the holes in the leather.

Stitch around the top of the dice box with blanket stitches, then stitch the vertical seam.

The seam up the side of the box and the seam joining the base to the sides should be sewn twice, as shown in the drawing.

MATERIALS:
- ● Two pieces of hard leather 4½ × 3 in.
- ● 3 ft. of silk cord
- ● Pieces of colored morocco
- ● PVA glue and cutting tools

MEDALLION

Make a pattern out of paper using the drawing on the right as a guide. Draw the outline on both pieces of leather and cut them out. On one of the pieces only, cut out three triangle-shaped holes.

Stick this piece of leather on top of the other. Then stick triangles of colored morocco in the holes cut out for them. Leave the medallion to dry under some books.

When the glue is dry, punch the holes around the edge for the cord.

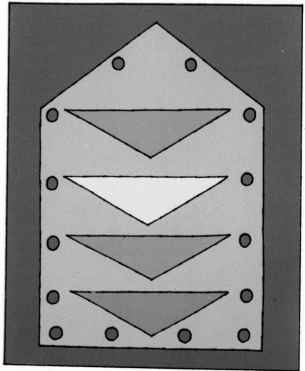

24

Tie a series of knots in the middle part of the cord. Pass the ends through the holes, starting at the top end and looping the cord around itself each time as shown in the drawing.

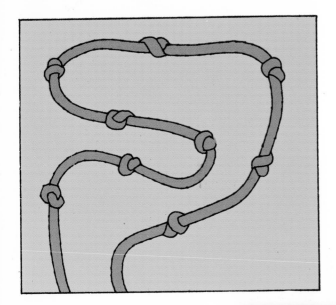

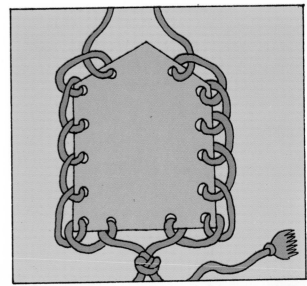

Tie the cord together at the bottom of the medallion. Tie a further knot in each of the ends.

MATERIALS:

- Piece of colored leather 10×3½ in.
- Piece of natural leather 12½×3½ in.
- Small pieces of leather in different colors
- Needle, thread and scissors

SCISSORS CASE

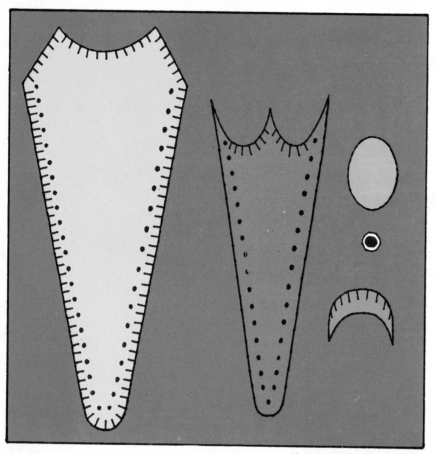

Cut out pieces of leather using the shapes in the drawing as a guide. The size depends on the size of the scissors for which the case is being made.

Stick the pieces which make up the eyes on the leather which forms the background. Make sure that the glue is really dry before you start sewing; it is best to leave the pieces for an hour or so under some books.

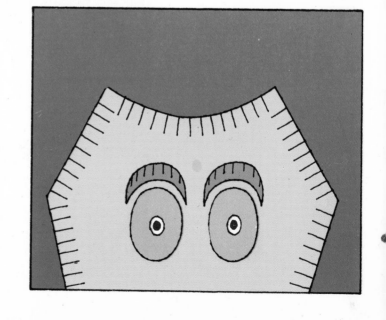

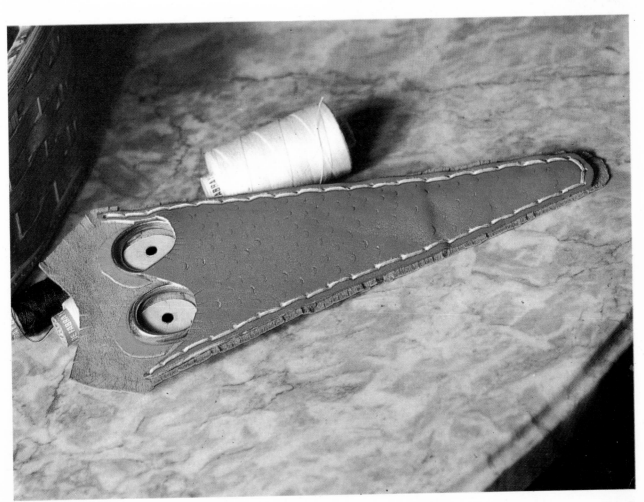

Sew along the seams as in the drawing.

MATERIALS:

- Two strips of morocco $12\frac{1}{2} \times \frac{3}{4}$ in. in different colors
- Small piece of morocco for the loop
- Buckle
- PVA glue
- Punch and bradawl

WATCH STRAP

Using the punch, make a series of holes in one of the pieces of morocco, $\frac{1}{2}$ in. apart.

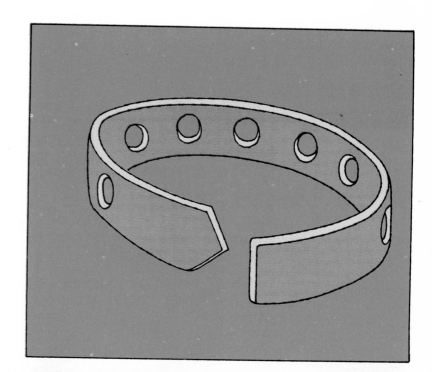

Stick the other strip to the one with holes in it; when the glue is completely dry, make three holes in the end of the strap with the bradawl.

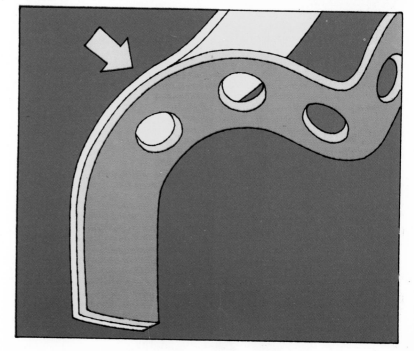

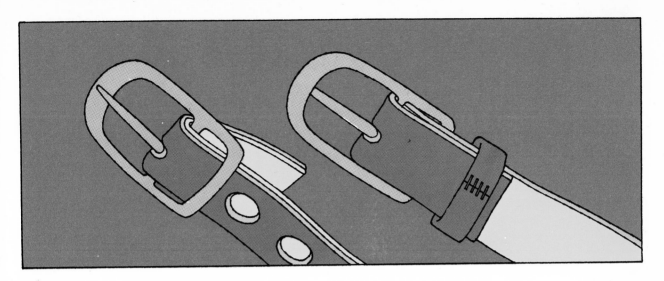

Sew the buckle to the other end of the strap. The stitches which fasten the buckle can also be used to attach the loop of morocco which holds the free end of the strap in place.

GLASSES CASE

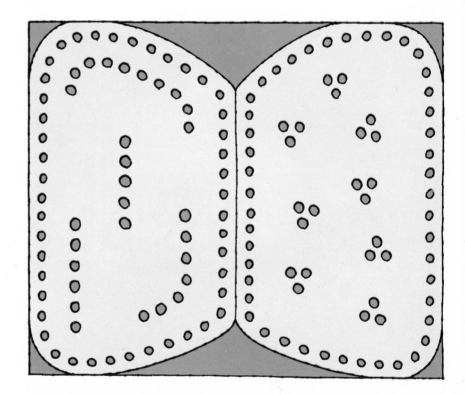

Cut out the two pieces of morocco to the pattern in the drawing. Use a pair of glasses as a guide for the exact size and shape. Punch out the holes around the edge leaving a space of ½ in. between each one. Punch out holes for the colored dots from the piece of thick morocco only. Punch out the dots from the small pieces of colored morocco. Place the lining beneath the thicker piece of morocco. Before placing each dot in position put a small amount of glue in the holes, and another small amount on the back of the dot. Then put the dot into the hole and press it well down.

You can also stick initials and other decorations into the case. Cut out the letters from the pieces of colored morocco, then draw the outline of the letters on the thick morocco with a sharp pencil. When all the dots and decorations are glued in place, leave under some books for about four hours, until the glue is completely dry.

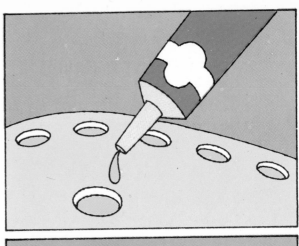

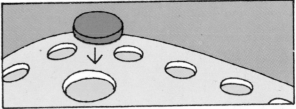

Then sew the edges together with the leather strip. To make it easier to thread the strip through the holes, stick a piece of self-adhesive tape to the end, and twist it into a point. When you have sewn round the edges, pass the end of the strip inside the case and fasten it with a drop of glue.

MATERIALS:

- Two pieces of green leather: one 10×5 in., one 6×1½ in. for the flap
- Piece of brown leather 8½×4 in.
- Piece of yellow leather 7½×3 in.
- Press stud, scissors
- Needle and thread

WALLET

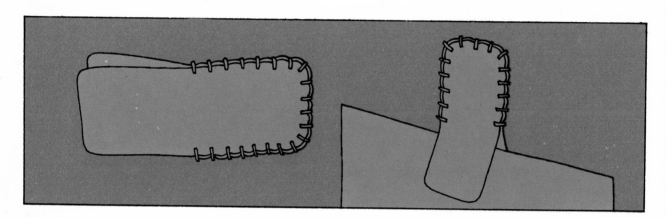

Cut the small green piece of leather in half widthways and sew the two pieces together with blanket stitches as shown in the drawing.

When you reach the middle of the flap, slot the two ends over the edge of the large piece of green leather. Continue stitching so that the flap is firmly fastened to the larger piece.

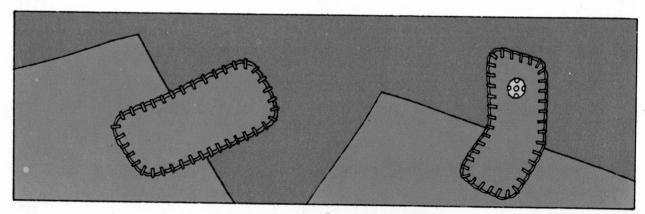

Sew one half of the press stud to the inside of the flap, making sure that the stitches only pass through one layer of leather, so that they are not seen on the outside. Sew the other half of the stud to the outside of the notecase.

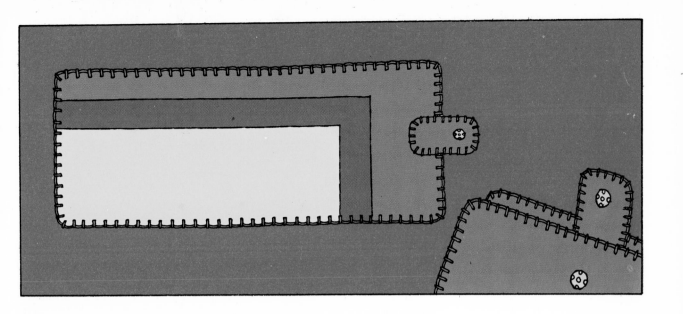

Place the yellow and brown pieces of leather in the bottom left hand corner of the green piece, and blanket-stitch around the edge so as to fasten the three pieces together. Continue the stitching right around the green piece to finish it off.

MATERIALS:
- Piece of leather $11 \times 5\frac{1}{2}$ in.
- Two pieces of morocco $5\frac{1}{2} \times 4\frac{1}{4}$ in. the same color as the leather
- Two pieces of stiff clear plastic $5\frac{1}{2} \times 4\frac{1}{4}$ in.
- PVA glue
- Scissors

PHOTO WALLET

The large piece of leather forms the outside of the wallet. Cut the pieces for the flap and fastener from the center of one of the pieces of morocco making sure that enough is left for the frame.

Stick the flap and fastener to opposite ends of the wallet, as in the drawing.

Cut the two frames from the pieces of morocco as shown, then stick the pieces of clear plastic to the inside of the frames. Finally, stick the frames and pieces of plastic together to the inside of the wallet, making sure that the edges match up exactly with those of the leather case. Stitch each of the frames on three sides only, leaving the fourth side, in the center of the wallet, open, to take the photograph. When you have stuck all the parts together, leave the wallet under some books for several hours to dry.

BOOK COVER

Cut the large piece of leather to the same depth as the book, and about 6 in. longer than the total width of the two covers plus the spine. Cut the smaller pieces of leather to the shape shown in the drawing.

Fold the two ends of the cover inwards and stick down the small pieces of leather to hold them in place. Leave the finished work under some books for several hours until the glue is completely dry.

MATERIALS:
- Pieces of morocco in different colors
- Square piece of hard leather
- Punch, scissors, PVA glue, knife

MEDALLION AND CHAIN

Cut 16 pieces of different colored morocco to the pattern shown on the left in the drawing. Thread these pieces together.

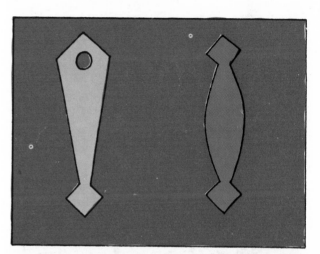

The square head of each piece is fitted into the hole in the next, and then fastened in place with a drop of glue.

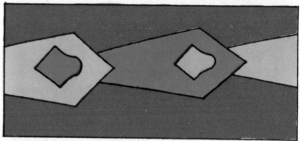

One piece, forming the 17th in the chain, should have two square heads instead of a hole. This links one end of the chain to the medallion.

Punch four holes in the medallion and push the ends of the chain through them as shown in the drawing.

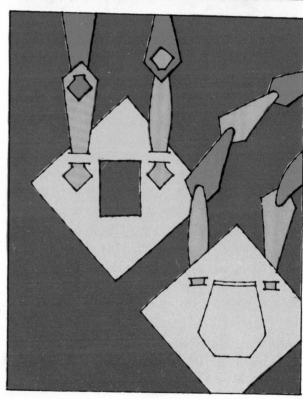

Make a rectangular hole in the center of the medallion, and cover the back of it with a small piece of morocco, stuck down on three sides. The top edge should be left open to take the photograph or drawing.

MATERIALS:

- Two pieces of soft leather $3\frac{1}{2} \times 3$ in. in two different colors
- Piece of soft leather $4\frac{1}{2} \times \frac{3}{4}$ in., for the tassel
- Key ring 1 in. in diameter
- 5 colored beads, scissors
- PVA glue, needle and thread
- Initials made of gold sticky tape

KEY RING

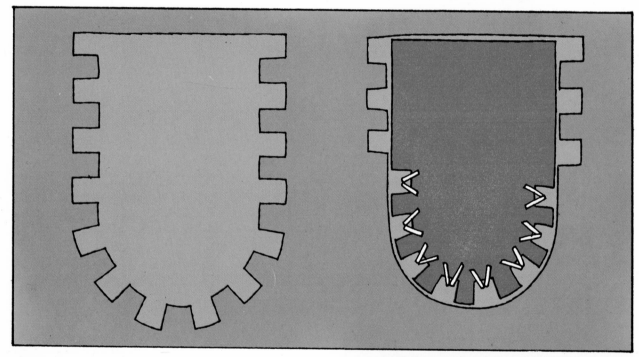

Measure the keys which are to be put on the ring and cut the leather so that they will fit into the pouch with a little room to spare. Cut the pieces of leather to the pattern shown in the drawing, one with tabs, the other without.

Then place one on top of the other and stick down the tabs, starting from the middle. Reinforce each tab with a couple of diagonal stitches as shown. Cut fringes in one end of the strip reserved for the tassel, making the tips very pointed so that they can be passed through the holes in the beads.

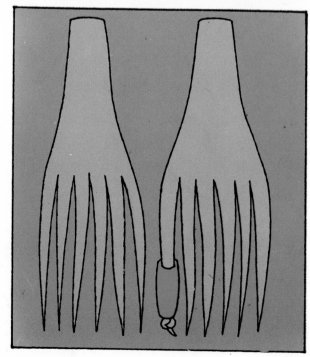

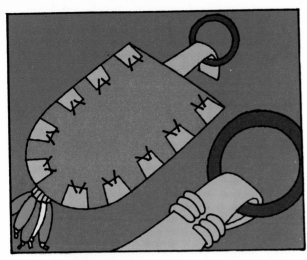

Thread the beads onto the fringes and tie a knot in the end of each one to prevent the beads from slipping off. The other end of the strip is passed through the center of the pouch, and the key ring is sewn onto it.
Now the key ring is ready for use.

BRACELET

Punch a hole in the round piece of leather, then arrange the colored pieces of leather around this hole as shown in the drawing. When you put the glue on the pieces, be careful not to use too much, as this may stain the leather background. When the decorations have been stuck in place, leave the disc under some books for an hour or so until the glue is completely dry.

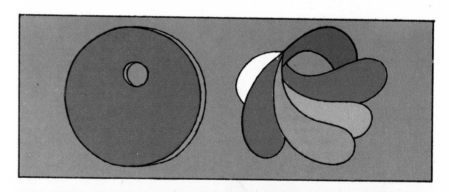

Pass the leather cord through the hole in the disc and pinch the piece of tin into the ends as shown, with a pair of pliers. Finally loop the cord through the clip and pinch this together to hold in place.

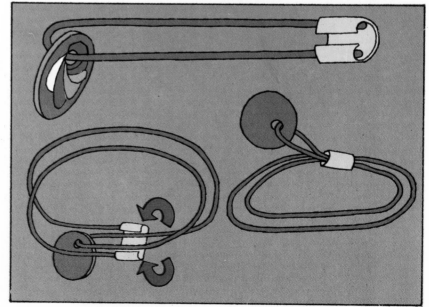

MATERIALS:

● Piece of leather 12½ × 8 in.
● Two pieces 4 × 5 in., for the stripes
● PVA glue, scissors
● Leather punch

TIGER

Cut out the different pieces using the shapes shown in the drawings as a guide. Punch holes in the pieces forming the eyes, to give the effect of pupils. Stick the mouth, eyebrows and eyes onto the face, and then the stripes onto the body.

When sticking each piece, especially if it is a small one, take great care that the glue does not spread out from the edges and stain the leather of the tiger's body. If this should happen wipe it up quickly with a clean rag.

After sticking on the final piece, place the tiger under some books for several hours until the glue is completely dry and all the stripes are stuck firmly in position.

BUTTONS

Using the knife, cut out the pieces of leather which will form the base of the buttons. These can be round, square, oblong or irregular in shape, but it is worth remembering that round buttons fasten the best and are least likely to damage the button holes. Loop a piece of wire through each base as shown in the drawing, so that the button can eventually be sewn onto clothing.

Cut the piece or pieces forming the decoration from leather of a different color from that of the base. The drawings show up to five different patterns, all made by sticking pieces of leather on top of the base. These pieces also hide the ends of the wire.

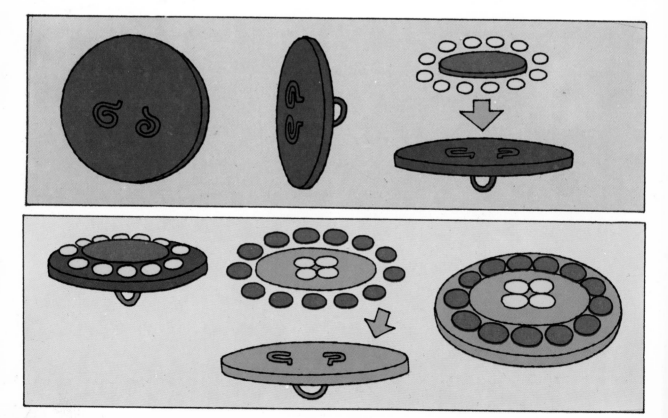

When the button is finished, give the whole surface a coating of PVA glue. This will help to hold the different pieces in place and also to bring out the colors of the leather.

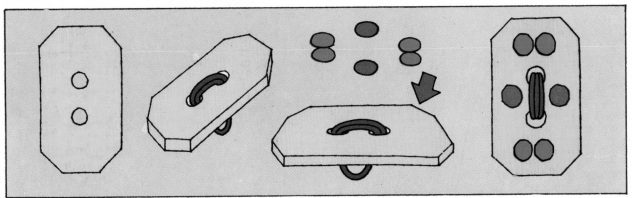

MATERIALS:

- Pieces of pony skin or leather in different colors
- Circular rivets or eyelets
- Metal buckle the same color as the rivets
- Leather punch, or eyeletting tool

BELT

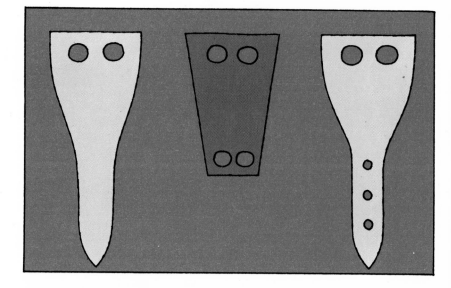

Cut the pieces of leather to the pattern shown in the center drawing above, then punch holes in them to take the rivets or eyelets. If pony skin is used, make sure that the hair on the skin goes in the same direction on all the pieces. Then rivet or eyelet the pieces together.

The pieces of skin should be arranged so that the colors go in a regular series, e.g. white, brown, black; white, brown, black; etc.

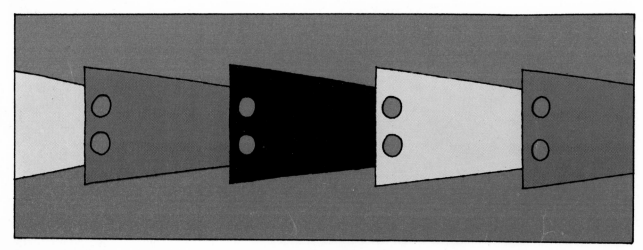

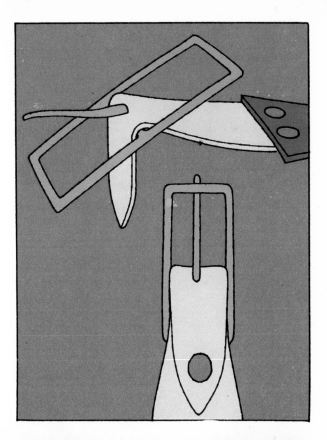

Now cut out the pieces which form the ends of the belt (see page 48, on the left and the right of the drawing). The piece on the right, with the holes punched into it, should be longer than the piece on the left.
The buckle is mounted on the smaller one as shown in the drawing on the right. The large piece is punched with holes to take the tongue of the buckle.

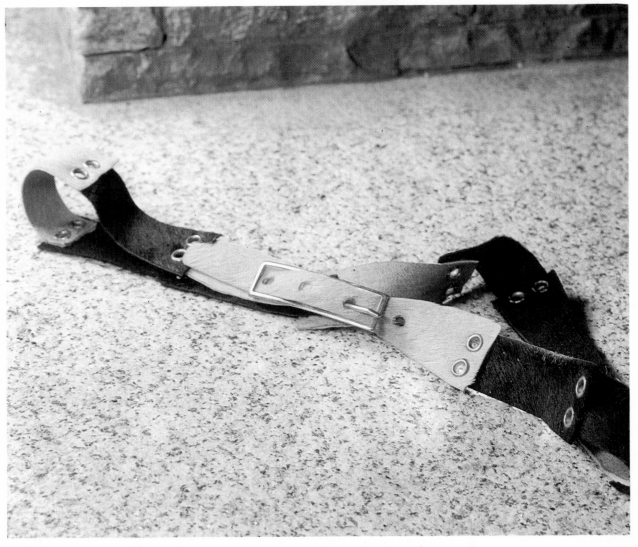

MATERIALS:

- Round piece of red morocco 7½ in. in diameter
- Round piece of red morocco 10 in. in diameter
- Piece of green morocco 5½×2½ in.
- Pieces of colored cloth
- Piece of white cloth 9×3 in.
- Scissors
- Needle and red thread
- Small amount of clean sand
- Foam rubber chips

SEWING CUSHION

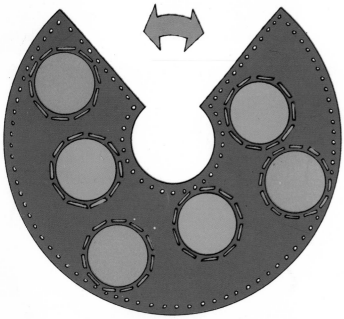

Cut the larger piece of red morocco to the pattern shown in the drawing above, and cut six holes in it. Sew the colored pieces of cloth to one side, stitching around each hole. Then sew the two ends together.

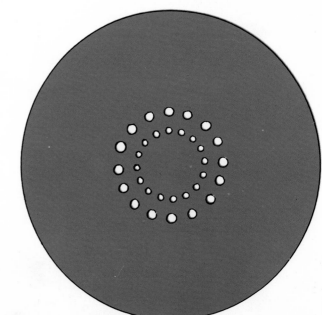

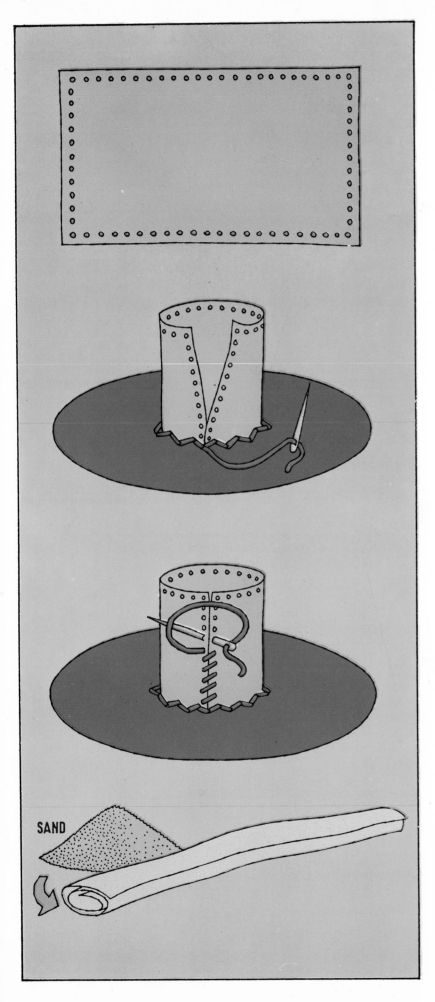

Sew the rectangle of green morocco to the center of the smaller piece of red morocco which forms the base, as shown. Then sew up the side of the rectangle so that it makes a cylinder.

Sew a piece of white cloth into a long, thin sausage, fill it with sand. Then sew the ends together to make a ring. This sand-filled ring is then placed around the cylinder of green morocco, where it will make the cushion heavier.

SAND

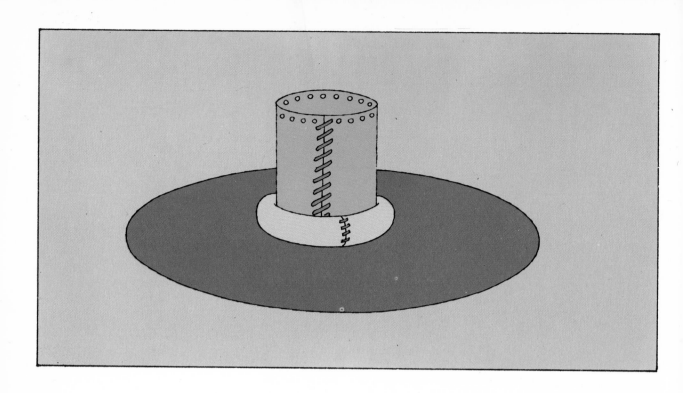

Place the part of the cushion you have already made over the base and sew the upper edge of the green cylinder to the opening at the top.

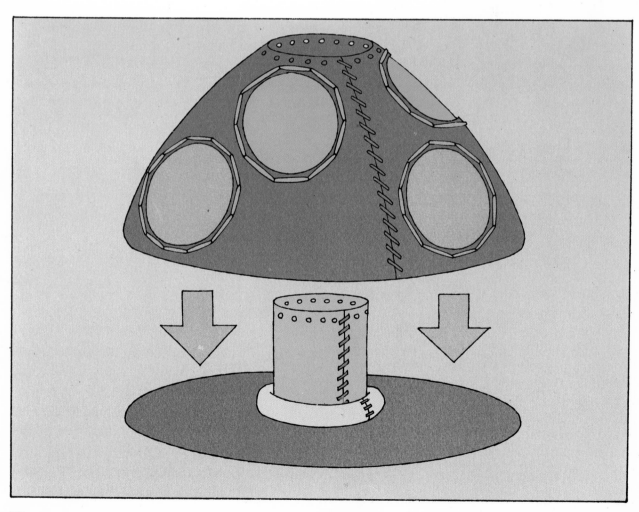

The base and upper part are then sewn together, leaving a small opening through which the cushion can be stuffed with foam rubber chips. Finally, sew up the opening and tie the thread securely.

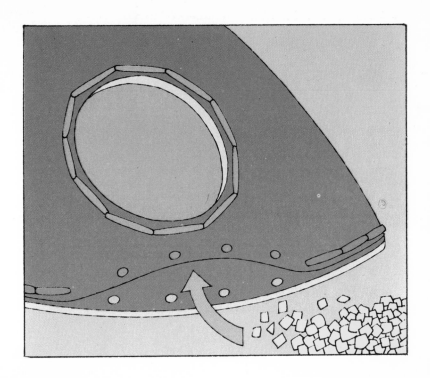

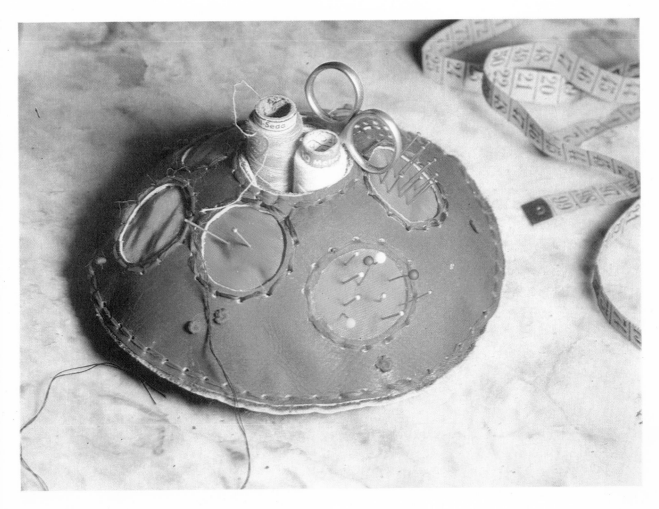

This cushion will be very useful for holding sewing materials: needles threaded with different colored cotton, pins, cotton reels and scissors.

PURSE

Cut the red suede to the pattern shown in the drawing.
Punch holes in the suede where you want to put the rivets. Arrange the different colored heads in more or less regular patterns.

Punch a line of holes along each edge and then sew the two halves together with the strip of red suede. At the end of each seam, pass the strip inside the purse and fasten it with a drop of glue.

To fix the mouth on the purse, smear some glue along the top edge of the suede and insert this into the metal channel. Pinch the edges of the channel together with pliers so that they firmly grip the leather. To avoid damaging the metal, place a piece of rag or soft leather between it and the teeth of the pliers.

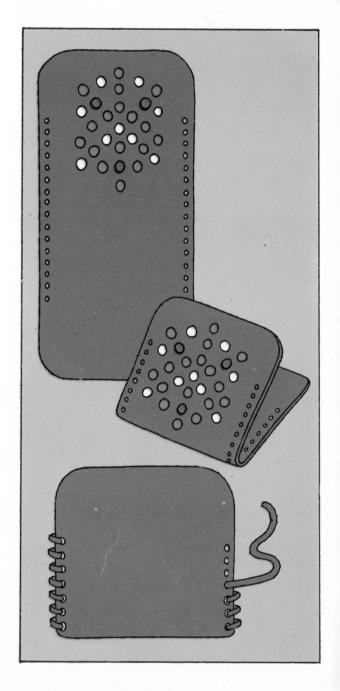

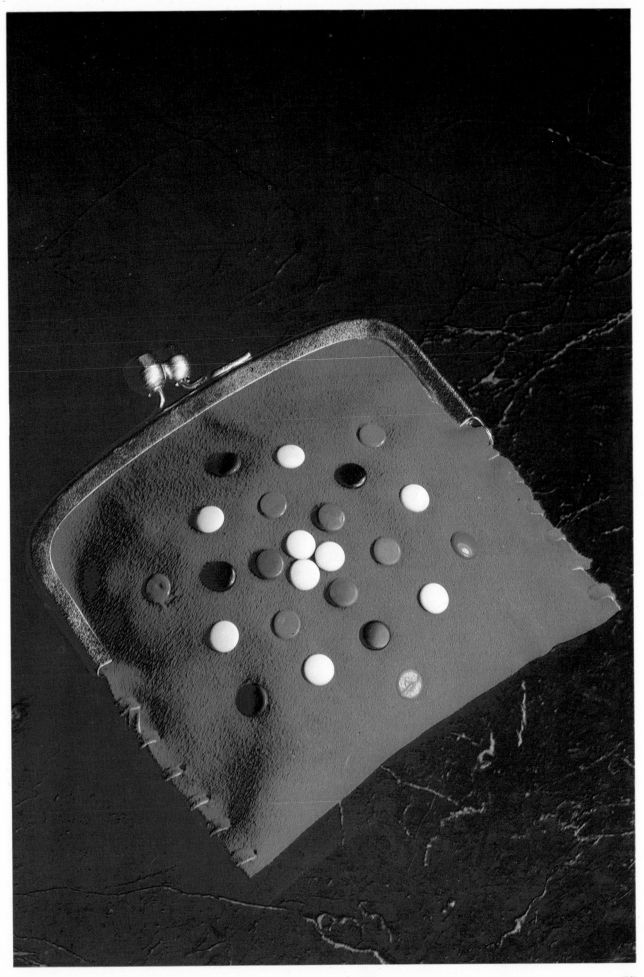

SHOE-CLEANING BAG

Cut the pieces to the patterns shown in the drawing. Punch holes along all the edges to take the thread for the seams and the strip of yellow morocco which decorates the top edge of the bag.

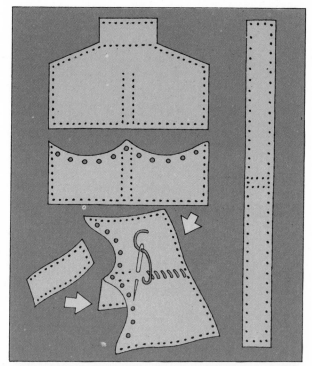

Using the bodkin and orange thread, stitch together the various pieces of the bag.

When sewing the $3 \times 5\frac{1}{2}$ in. piece of morocco which forms the division between the two parts of the bag, the stitches should be made loosely so as not to pull the leather out of shape.

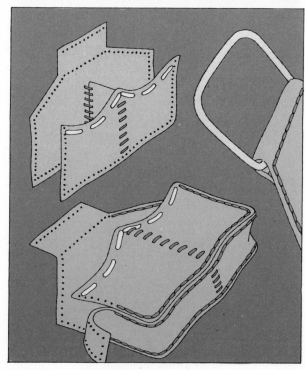

When the front and back of the bag have been joined by this piece, sew on the strip which forms the bottom and the sides.

Fix the handle to the back of the bag by doubling over the flap at the top and sewing it together with broad stitches.

Fasten the colored morocco decorations in place with a drop of glue.

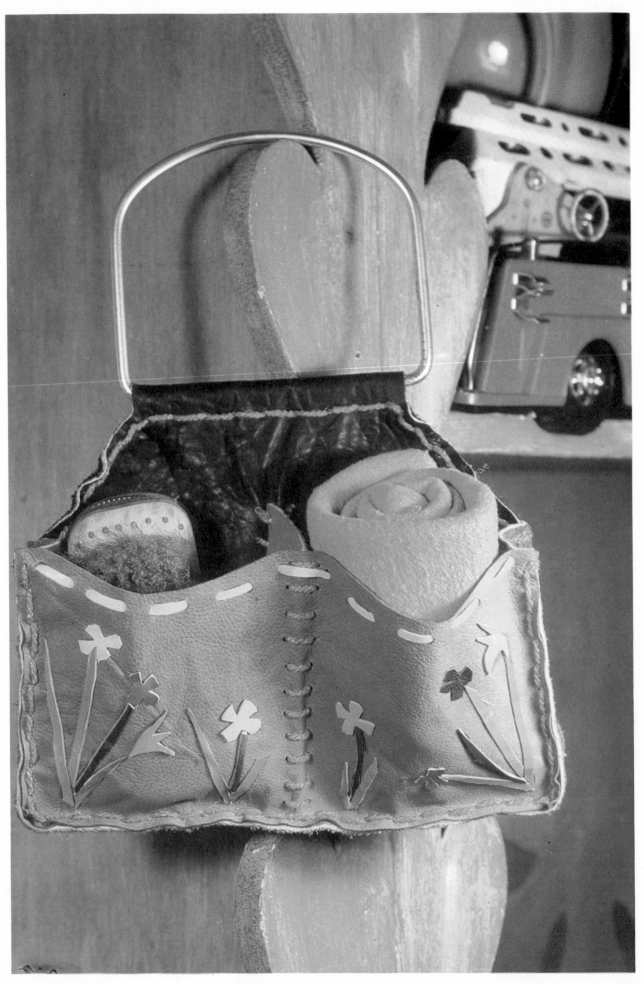

MATERIALS:
- Pieces of soft leather in different colors
- Board 27×13½ in., ring and staple
- PVA glue, scissors
- Cream-colored paint

LEAVES

Cut out the pieces of leather for the different parts of each leaf. The best way of doing this is to draw the whole leaf first on a sheet of paper and cut this into pieces. The pieces of paper can then be used as a pattern for the different parts of the leaf, which should each be cut from leather of a different color.

The strips of leather which form the veins should be made in light colors so that they stand out against the darker colors of the leaves.

Now stick the pieces of each leaf down on the board with glue. It does not matter if the glue spreads a little around the edges of the leaf, since any minor stains will be covered by the paint.

When the leaves are stuck to the wood and the glue is quite dry, paint all the visible parts of the board; take great care and use a very fine brush to paint around the edges of the leaves, making sure that you do not get any paint on the leather.

Drive the staple with its ring into the top end of the board so that the finished work can be hung on the wall. If you wish, you can trim the board by sticking a strip of braid around the edge.

BRACELET

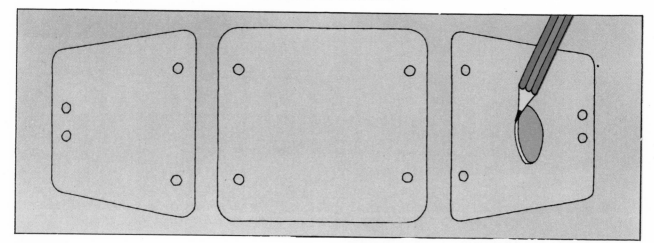

Cut the three parts of the bracelet from the leather, as shown in the drawing, then punch the holes which will take the wire.

Place each gem in the position it will occupy on the leather and draw around it with a sharp pencil, without pressing too hard. Using a scalpel, cut around $\frac{1}{2}$ in. inside the pencil line as shown in the drawing. Do not go too deep into the leather—just enough so that by hollowing out the cut slightly you can fit the base of the stone into the depression.

Put some glue on the leather and on the base of the stone and stick it into the hollow. When all the gems are stuck in position, you can start making the wire links. Cut 4 pieces of wire $2\frac{1}{2}$ in. long and flatten them out by hammering them on a piece of iron.

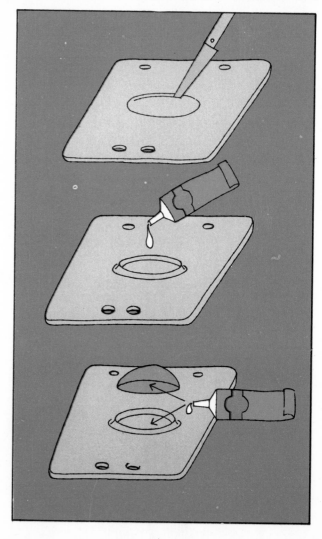

Bend them into a loop as shown in the drawing and pass them through the holes to join the pieces of leather to one another.

Flatten some more wire to make the clasp shown at the top of the drawing, which is fastened to either end of the bracelet.

To decorate the bracelet, mark circles on the leather with the punch so that they only just cut into the surface; to make these decorations stand out, give the whole bracelet a coating of blue or green dye.

The bracelet can also be made in dyed leather, and the decoration treated with darker dye to make it stand out.

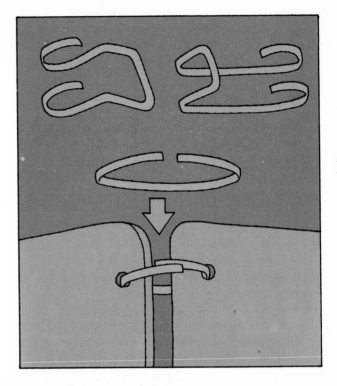

FISH

Cut out the different pieces from the colored morocco. Punch holes in the body of the fish. These holes will be filled with small pieces of morocco in different colors.

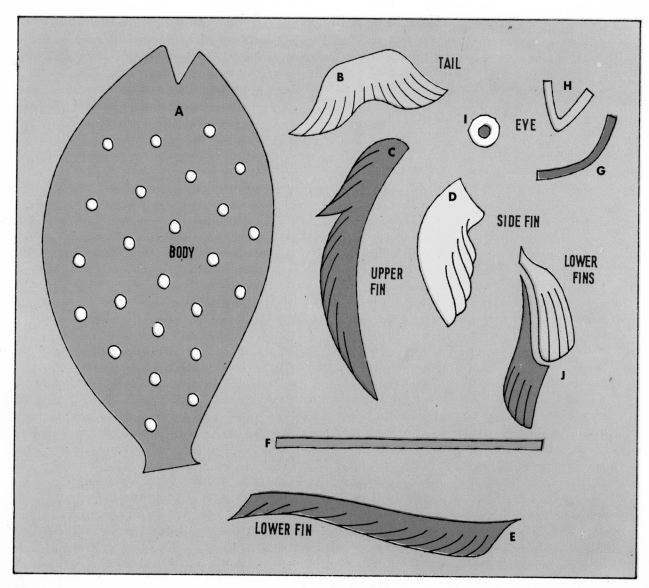

Paint the lid of the cardboard box. When the paint is completely dry, stick the pieces of the fish on top. Instead of filling some of the holes in the fish with pieces of colored morocco, leave some of them open, so that the paint on the lid shows through them.

You could also use some of the round pieces of morocco to decorate the lid.

Once the pieces of leather are stuck on, you can use other colors for the painted background.

MATERIALS:

- Piece of hard leather 6 × 3½ in.
- 8 colored gems
- 12 ft. of suitable wire
- PVA glue, punch and knife

NECKLACE

Cut five pieces out of the leather to the pattern shown in the drawing. Make punch marks on the polished surface of the leather, then mark the places where the stones are to be set.

⅛ in. inside the first circular mark, make another similar mark, cutting a little more deeply into the leather. The leather inside the second mark should then be removed. Cut the area between the two circles into six segments, leaving a tiny space between each one.

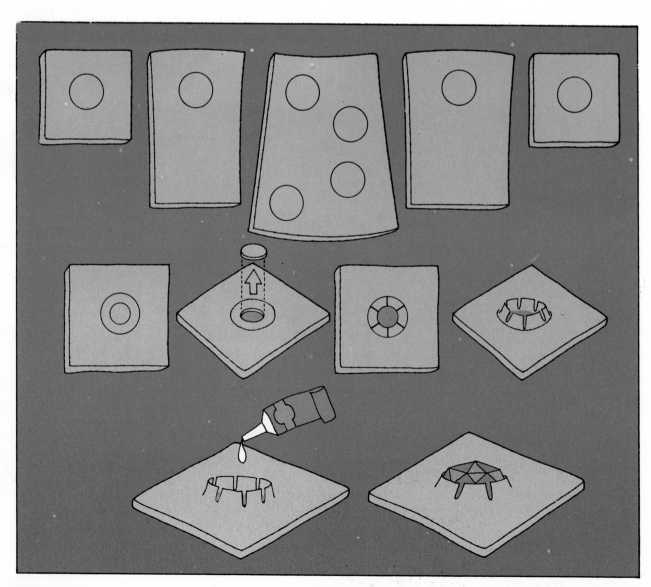

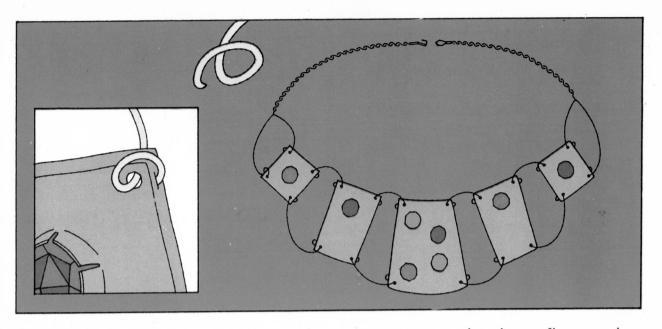

Raise these tabs very carefully and set the stones under them, first putting some glue on the leather underneath to keep them securely in place. Join together the pieces of leather with lengths of wire shaped as shown in the drawing. When positioning these, make sure that the end of the wire is stuck firmly into the edge of the leather so that it does not scratch the neck of the wearer.

Make the chain of the necklace from two lengths of wire. Form one of these ends into a small ring and the other into a hook, which join together to form the clasp of the necklace.

SHOULDER BAG

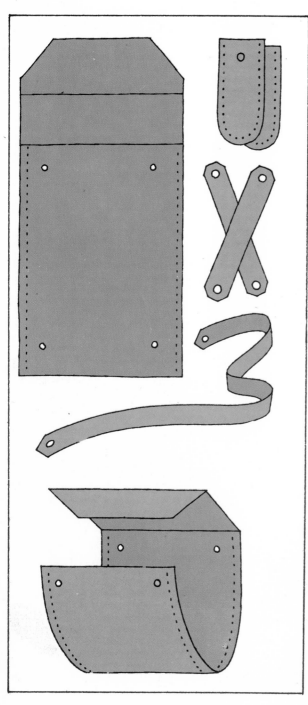

Cut the various pieces to the pattern shown in the drawing. On the pieces which have to be perforated (to take the thread for the seams), mark a line $\frac{1}{4}$ in. in from the edge and use this as a guide when punching the holes. It is advisable to shave down the leather on the edges which are to be sewn, so that the seams will fit together better.

Punch the holes to take the rivets for the two straps which fasten over the top.
Using the bradawl, score heavily along the two lines where the top will fold over.
Punch holes in the two pieces forming the sides to take the rivets for the shoulder straps.

Use a pair of dividers to mark the circular patterns decorating the top of the bag. The smaller circles are made with the leather punch, which is pressed into the leather just enough to leave a mark. Take care not to cut right through the leather.

When all the holes have been punched and the decorations marked on the bag, prepare the dye and coat all the pieces of leather with it, making sure that it soaks well into the scored

MATERIALS:

- Piece of hard leather 34 × 21 in.
- Fabric dye in a dark color
- Four large rivets
- Two small rivets
- Knife
- Two stout needles, strong thread
- Leather punch and bradawl

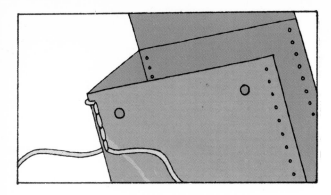 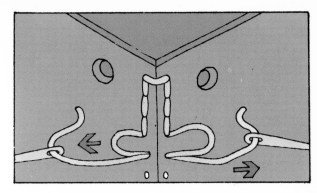

patterns so that they stand out as a dark outline. When the dye has dried, use the four large rivets to attach the straps which fasten the top, and the two smaller rivets for the shoulder strap.

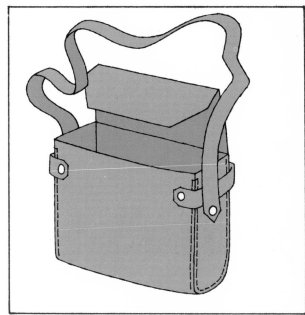

Lastly, sew together the three main parts of the bag; the seams are done with two needles at the same time, as shown in the drawing, so that the stitches are perfectly even on both sides.

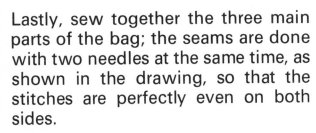

WOVEN MAT

Weave together the strips of leather as shown in the drawing, making sure that two of the same color do not come together.

Fix the ends of each strip with a drop of glue so that the mat does not move while you are punching the holes for the narrow strip which fastens the edges

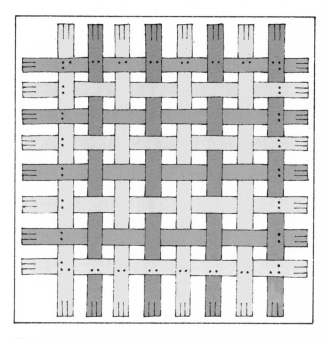

In order to thread the strip of morocco through the holes, wrap a piece of adhesive tape around one of the ends to stiffen it and twist this into a point.

Knot the strips together at the corners so that they hold the mat together, but be careful not to pull them too tight.

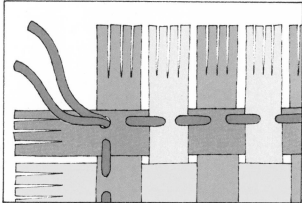

Finally, cut fringes in the end of each leather strip.

This mat can be used as a decoration and also as a table mat for plates or flowerpots.

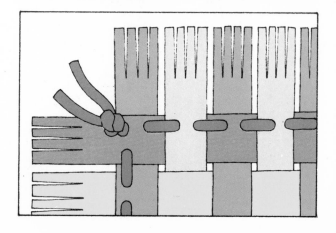

MATERIALS:

● **Soft yellow leather**
● **Soft natural leather for 20 thongs on the shoulders and loops to fasten the toggles**
● **Leather punch**
● **Needle**
● **Thread**
● **Scissors**

VEST

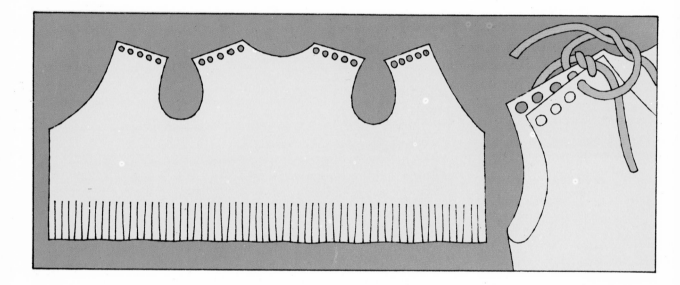

Cut the vest from the yellow leather, all in one piece as shown in the drawing. Cut fringes along the bottom edge.

Punch 10 holes along each of the shoulders to take the leather thongs. Each of the thongs is approximately 12 in. long. They are threaded through the holes in the two edges which form the shoulder and tied in a simple knot; the loose ends then fall in a fringe over the shoulder.

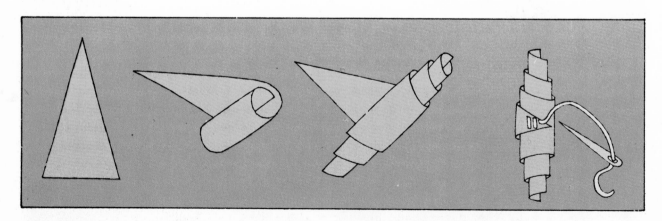

The toggles are made from a triangular piece of leather which is rolled up and then fastened with a couple of stitches on the outside.

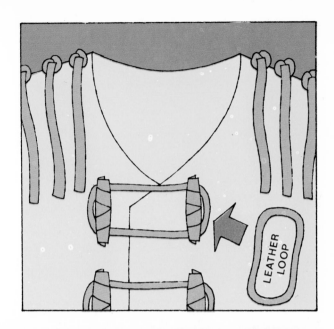

The six toggles are all the same, as are the three loops of leather which hook over the toggles to fasten the vest.

MATERIALS
- **Nine strips of leather in different colors, $\frac{1}{4}$ in. wide**
- **Copper ring $1\frac{1}{4}$ in. in diameter**
- **Sheet of copper $10 \times 6\frac{1}{2}$ in.**

PLAITED CORD

Plaiting strips of leather into a cord is a simple job which only requires a small amount of skill and practice. It is as well to experiment a little beforehand and make sure you have mastered the technique before embarking on the final job. If you have not tried this before, you should start with a cord of five strands. Then you can go on to seven, nine, or more; the number should always be an odd one, and the method is the same in each case.

The drawings show how to move the strands, which are each given a different color. It is advisable to use colored strands in practice, particularly for your first attempts; if possible, use the same colors as in the drawings, as this will make it easier to follow the instructions. Each strand has also been given a number, so that they are easier to identify if you are using strands of the same color.

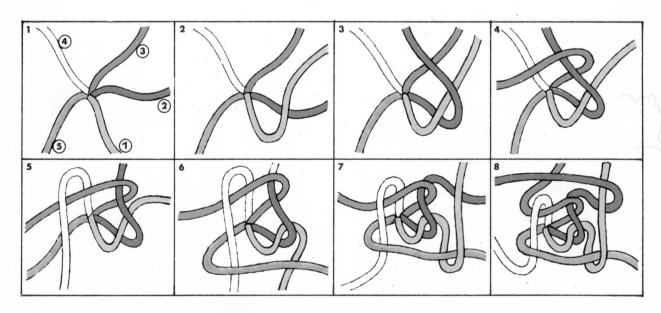

To begin the cord, knot the ends of the strands together. Then the order of working for a cord of five strands is as follows: green (1) over red (2); red (2) over green (1) and blue (3); blue (3) over red (2) and white (4); white (4) over blue (3) and orange (5); orange (5) over white (4) and green (1); green (1) over orange (5) and red (2); red (2) over green (1) and blue (3); blue (3) over red (2) and white (4); white (4) over blue (3)

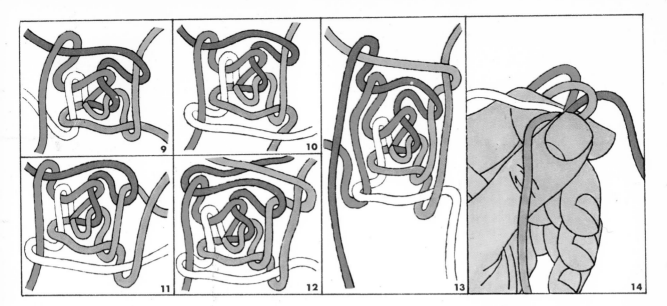

and orange (5); orange (5) over white (4) and green (1); green (1) over orange (5) and red (2); red (2) over green (1) and blue (3) . . .

By this time it will be obvious that the method is always the same: pass the second strip which is hanging down over the next two.

The work should be held in the left hand with the strands being plaited held between the thumb and forefinger.

The plaited cord hangs in the hollow of the left hand and must be turned continually so that the strands being plaited always hang over the forefinger of the left hand.

The attractive letter carrier shown in the photograph is hung from a nine-stranded cord. A copper ring was knotted to the top of the cord before the plaiting was started. Part of the way down, the cord is divided into three parts, which a little farther down separate into the nine strands, from which the copper plate is suspended. This plate has been hammered into a slight curve at the edges and has holes in it to take the strands, which are then knotted underneath.

Before starting, moisten the leather strips to make them supple, and you will then find it easier to plait the cord regularly.

MATERIALS
- Two pieces of green suede, each 20×10 in.
- Piece of green leather 12½×10 in.
- Piece of yellow morocco for the letters
- Wire coathanger
- Needle and thread
- PVA glue

COAT HANGER WITH POCKET

Cut out the two pieces of suede which are to cover the coat hanger. The best way of doing this is to lay the hanger on the back of the suede and draw around the edge with a sharp pencil.

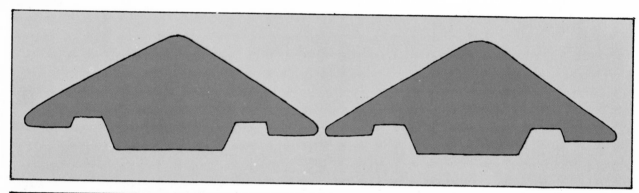

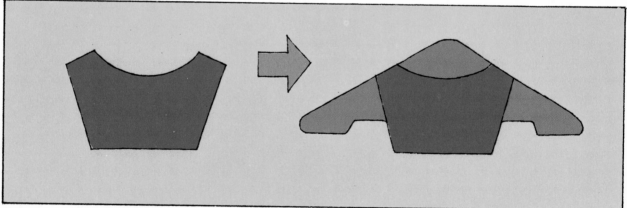

Then cut around the outline ½ in. out from the pencil line. This margin is left so that the seam does not come right on the edge of the leather, and thus lessens the danger of the leather tearing if it is pulled at.

The two identical pieces are then placed face to face and sewn together with broad stitches along the top two edges. The top edges of the piece of leather forming the pocket should also be sewn into these seams.

74

When you have finished sewing, turn the suede inside out so that the stitches are on the inside of the cover. Sew the green piece of leather onto the front of the cover to make the sides and the bottom of the pocket. The top is left open so that small objects can be easily inserted.

On the front of the pocket, stick the letters forming the name or initials of the person who is going to use the hanger.

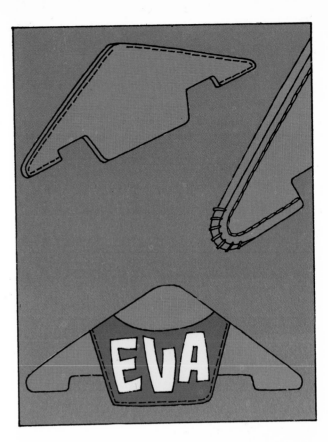

MATERIALS:

- Piece of flexible, undyed leather $27\frac{1}{2} \times 1\frac{3}{4}$ in.
- Piece of flexible brown leather $26\frac{1}{2} \times 1\frac{1}{2}$ in.
- Decorative metal shapes as available
- Buckle
- D-shaped ring
- Clip fastener
- Linen thread and stout needle
- Leather punch, PVA glue
- Five leather thongs: three 6 ft. long and two 5 ft. long

DOG COLLAR

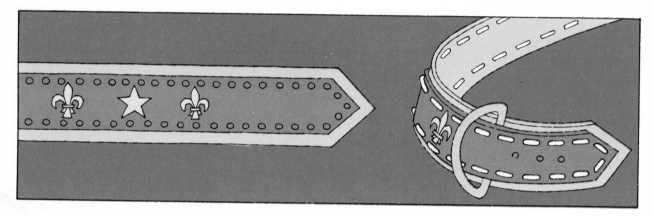

Mount the decorations on the strip of brown leather. Then place this on top of the piece of natural leather and stick them together with a few drops of glue. This is merely to make it easier to punch the holes for sewing them together.

Sew the two strips together with linen thread, first inserting the D-ring under the brown strip of leather so that the two seams hold it in place.

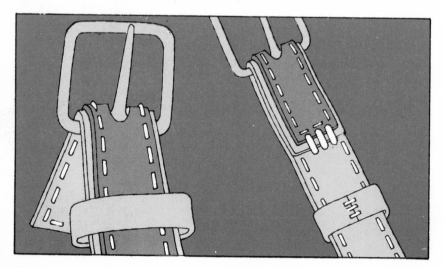

Punch a hole in one end of the collar, and sew on the buckle. Punch holes to take the tongue in the other end of the collar. Sew a loop of undyed leather $1\frac{1}{2}$ in. along from the buckle.

76

To make the lead, tie the five leather thongs together as shown and plait them by the method shown on page 72. For variety, you can leave some of the thongs unplaited at different points along the lead.

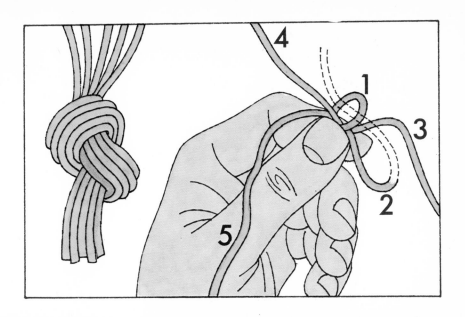

SHOULDER BAG

Cut a piece from the suede as shown in the drawing. Punch holes for the side seams, and also for the fringes at the bottom of the bag.

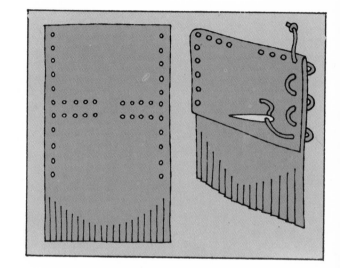

Sew the sides together, as shown, with the cord. Put a simple knot at one end, and form part of the shoulder strap with the other end (see below).

Stick the piece of hard leather inside the bag, just at the bottom of the flap. This will stiffen the opening.

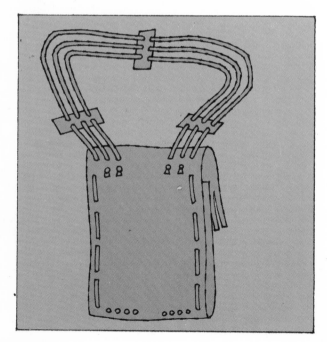

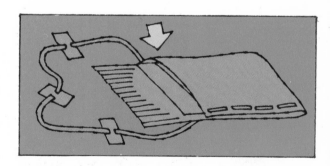

Complete the shoulder strap with more pieces of leather cord. Thread them through pieces of suede placed at regular intervals, to keep them more or less parallel.

MATERIALS:

- Natural-colored soft leather
- Leather laces in the same color
- Small pieces of morocco for the tassels
- Linen thread and stout needle
- Punch and PVA glue

MOCCASINS

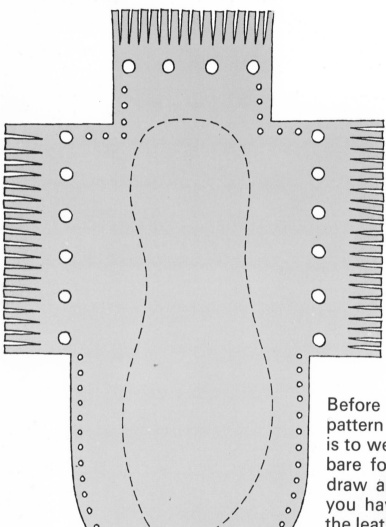

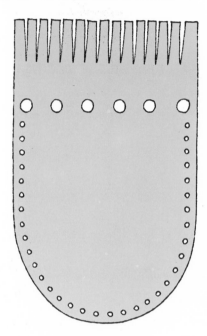

Before cutting the leather make a pattern of the sole of the person who is to wear the moccasins. Place their bare foot on a piece of paper and draw around it with a pencil. Once you have the pattern, place this on the leather and mark out the shape of the bottom piece of the moccasin around it, keeping to the proportions shown in the drawing on the left.

The upper part of the moccasin (the drawing on the right of this page) is exactly the same width as the foot, and its length is the distance between the big toe and the front of the ankle. Then punch the holes for the seams and the laces.

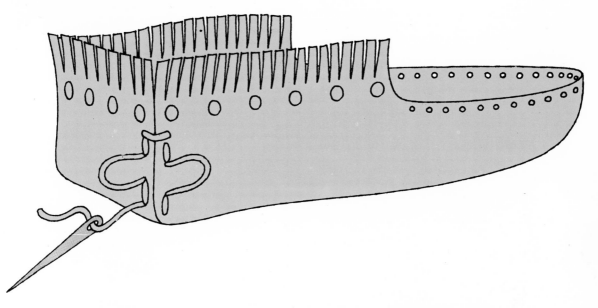

Sew the seams at the heel, and that which joins the upper part of the moccasin to the lower half. Use saddle stitches to do this in either of two ways: sewing with two needles simultaneously, or sewing in one direction first and then returning in the opposite direction, filling the spaces left by the first row of stitches.

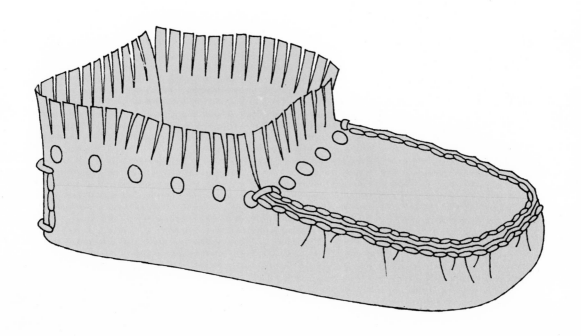

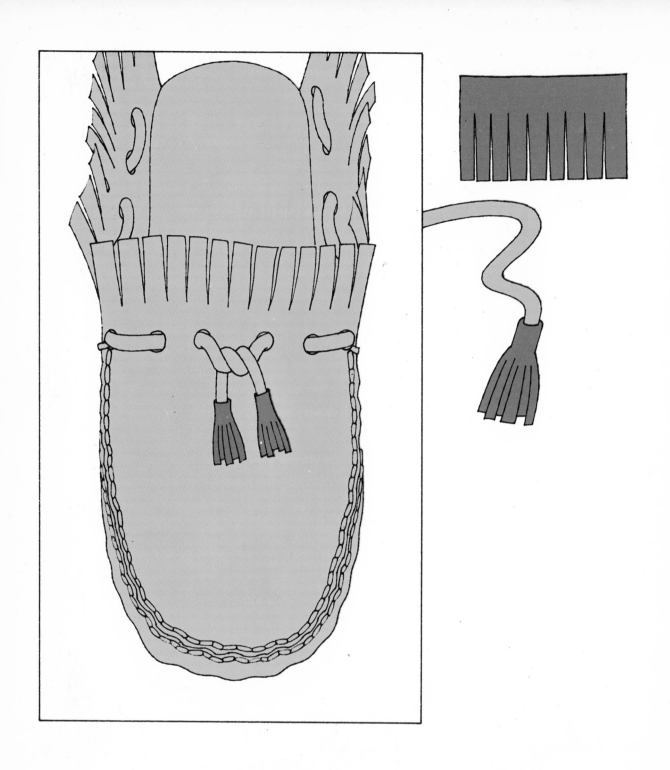

When the whole moccasin is sewn together, thread the lace through the holes and attach the tassels to the ends. The tassels are made from rectangles of morocco with a fringe cut along one edge; these are rolled around the end of the lace after applying glue to the part above the fringe.

Use the laces to draw the moccasin tight around the ankle.

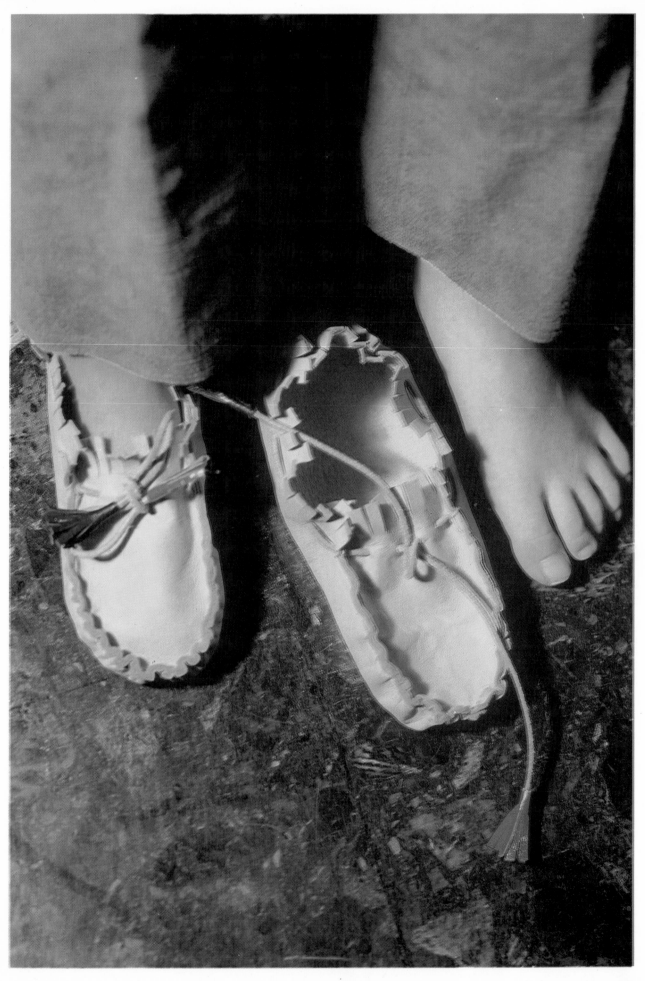

MATERIALS:

- A stone
- Pieces of soft leather in different colors
- Silver and copper wire
- Leather punch, hammer
- PVA glue
- Needle and thread

PAPERWEIGHT

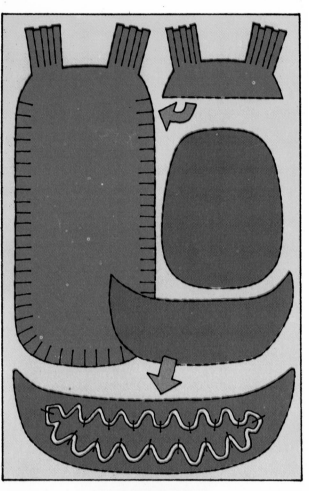

Cut the pieces from soft leather of different colors.

The blue piece shown in the drawing forms the underside of the weight and also the ears. The ears are made double so that the back of the leather is not exposed.

From the brown leather, or whatever other color you wish, cut the pieces forming the top of the head, the mouth and the two sides.

Bend the silver wire into the shape required for the teeth, then beat it flat with the hammer. The teeth are then sewn onto the front of the piece forming the mouth and sides.

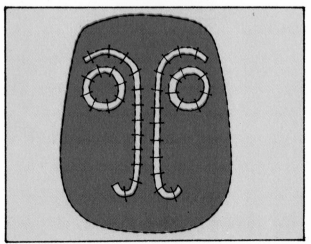

The nose and eye pieces are made in the same way from copper wire, and then sewn onto the leather which forms the top of the head, in the appropriate place.

Stick the pieces onto the stone, using plenty of glue and holding each piece in place until it dries, so that it follows the shape of the stone. Stick pieces of white and green leather in the center of the copper circles to make the eyes.

Then stick on the strips of red leather which form the lips and also hide the join between the two pieces of brown leather. The spots on the nose are made with the leather punch. Finally, cut a piece of yellow leather into a fringe and stick it to the top of the head.

Tie-dyeing and Batik

TIE-DYEING

This is always done with commercial dyes which need heating, and these can be obtained from a druggist or hardware shop. Each brand will have instructions on the packet, and you should follow these when using the dye. It may be necessary to add salt at this stage.

All designs are made by tying the cloth before dipping it into the dye; the knots prevent the dye from penetrating, so that the tied parts retain their original color. It is essential to use enough dye so that you can move the cloth around in the liquid.

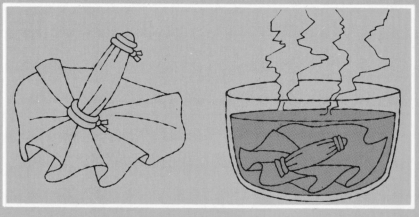

When the cloth is dyed, rinse it thoroughly and follow any other instructions on the packet.

When carrying out work in several colors, you should tie the parts of the cloth which are to keep the color they already have as tightly as possible; otherwise a second dipping will darken the parts which have been already dyed.

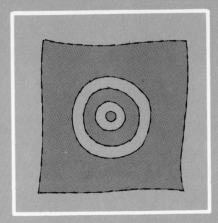

The background of the work, that is the parts of the cloth which have not been tied and have been through all the different baths of dye, will be a dark color resulting from the number of different colors used. A larger or smaller quantity of dye in the same amount of water will produce a lighter or darker tone of the same color.

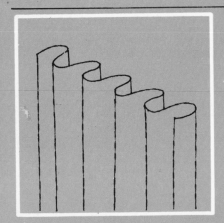 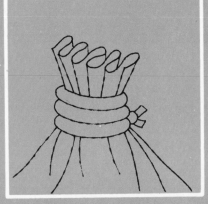 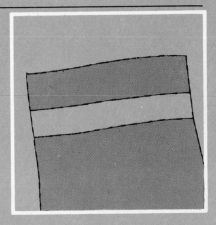

There are various ways of tying the cloth, giving many different patterns; here are some examples:

1. Stripes of color. Fold the cloth as shown in the drawing and bind it with lengths of thick white cotton. The cotton should cover the whole of the area to be protected from the dye.

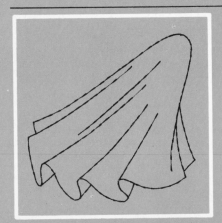  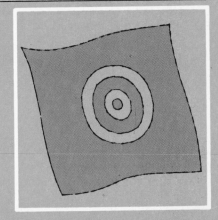

2. Concentric circles. Draw the cloth into a conical shape as shown in the drawing and bind the areas to be protected from the dye with cotton. If you want the circles to be perfectly concentric, pleat the cloth regularly, so that the color does not come out darker in some places than in others. You can get a different effect by pleating unevenly.

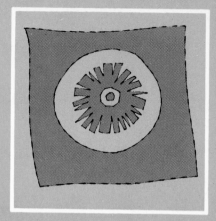

3. Radiating stripes. Gather the cloth as for the previous pattern, but instead of tying the cotton in bands, use a single thick strand running up the whole of the tied part (as shown in the drawing). Bring it back to the base in a crisscross fashion and knot it at the point at which you started.

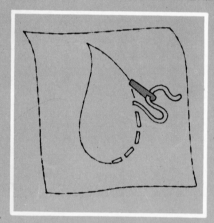

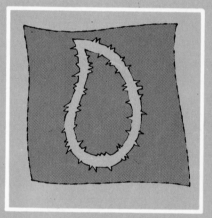

4. Outlines. Using white cotton, stitch loosely along the outline you wish to reproduce, then pull the thread so that the cloth is puckered and drawn together. Knot the ends of the cotton and then dip the cloth into the dye. The parts of the cloth held by the stitches will remain undyed or of a much lighter color than the rest of the cloth.

If the design to be reproduced is symmetrical, the cloth can be folded in two and stitched so that the same pattern appears on both halves. This can best be done with fairly large designs.

BATIK

The batik work shown here is carried out on white linen cloth, batiste or synthetic felt of the kind used for interlining. This kind of work can also be carried out on other types of cloth, such as silk or wool, but the methods and dyes used are different. Either beeswax or paraffin wax is used to impregnate the cloth and protect it from the dye. Beeswax gives a softer effect than paraffin wax which is used when a cracked effect is desired. The wax is placed in a double saucepan or with the wax container set in a saucepan of water over a low flame. It should be removed when the wax has melted, but before it begins to smoke, since if it is very hot it loses most of the properties needed for the work.

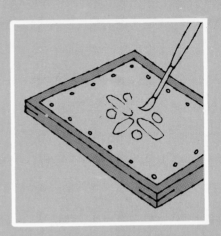

Apply the wax to the cloth with an ordinary brush making sure that it soaks right through the material. You will find it convenient to stretch the cloth on a frame so that it does not move while you are working on it. The brushes used for applying the wax should be cleaned with almost boiling water immediately after use.

The dyes used for this work are the so-called cold dyes. Before dyeing, rinse the cloth in cold water. A concentrated solution of dye must be used in order to produce vivid colors. It does not matter if the solution is lukewarm, but hot dyes cannot be used as they would dissolve the wax on the cloth. Follow the manufacturer's instructions carefully. It may be necessary to add salt and soda to the dye-bath.

When the cloth has been dyed, it should be rinsed and left to dry (do not wring).

Then place it between two clean sheets of blotting paper and pass a hot iron over the top until the paper has absorbed all the wax, leaving the cloth clean. If it proves difficult to remove all traces of wax from a piece of cloth, the best thing to do is send it to the cleaners to be dry cleaned. The use of solvents such as benzine is not recommended as they are highly inflammable.

PLACEMAT AND COASTERS

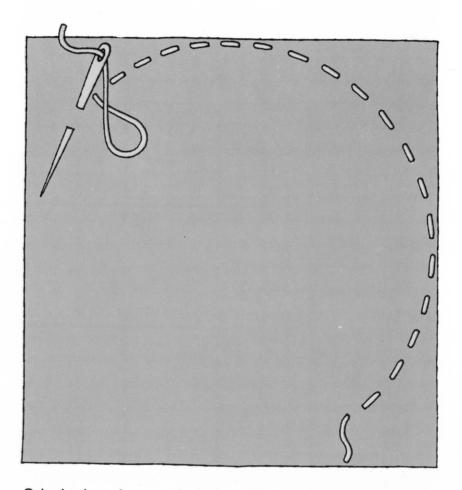

Stitch the pieces of cloth with the white cotton as shown in the drawing. Then draw the stitches together to form the base for the tying. Take care to fold the cloth as regularly as possible so that the dyeing comes out as a concentric and almost symmetrical pattern.

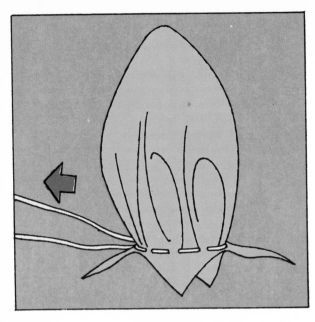

When all the pieces to be dyed have been tied dip them in the bath of dye (see page 86), moving them around in it to make sure that they are soaked right through and absorb the color properly. Then rinse them. Pull out a few threads around the edges of each piece to form a fringe. It can be held in place by a row of stitches.

T SHIRT

Tie the front of the T shirt as shown in the drawing; this will produce the circular design on the chest.

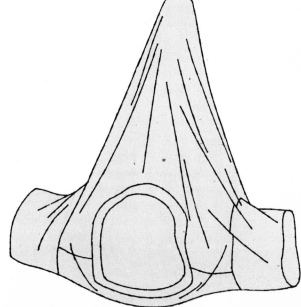

The band around the waist is produced by tying three turns of cotton very close together. The stripes around the sleeves are produced in the same way.

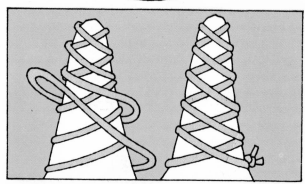

After dyeing, rinse the T shirt (see page 86) and leave it to dry.

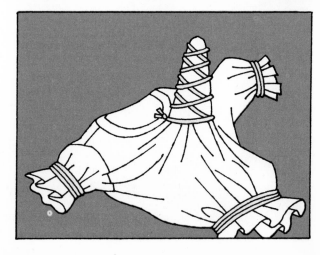

MATERIALS:

- Piece of white towelling 70 × 25 in.
- 18 ft. of white tape
- White cotton thread, dye
- Five small orange beads
- Two large orange beads

BEACH DRESS

Tie the towelling at the center and at the ends as shown in the drawing, making sure that you fold the cloth regularly so as to produce a regular pattern after dyeing.

The garment will have a circular pattern in the center, which will have a hole cut in it for the neck. A smaller circular pattern and two broad stripes decorate the front, while the back has four stripes.

 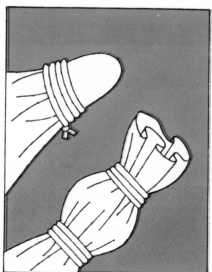 

As the towelling takes a long time to absorb water, you will need to leave it in the bath of dye for some time and stir it thoroughly, so that the dye soaks right in and the color is evenly distributed.

After dyeing, rinse the cloth, untie the thread and leave it to dry. When it is quite dry, cut the opening for the head and hem it on the inside.

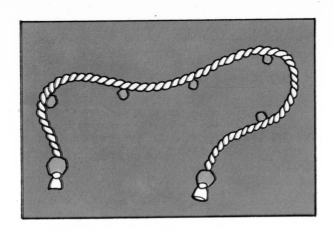

Sew the white tape all around the edge of the garment.
To make the belt, plait six pieces of the cotton thread used for tying into a cord, inserting the smaller orange beads at intervals along its length. Fasten the two large beads at each end of the cord.

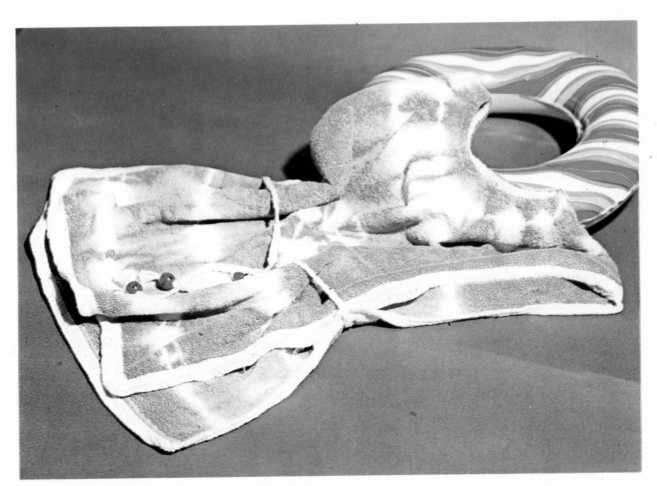

HANDKERCHIEF

Draw the pattern to be dyed on the cloth with a soft pencil.

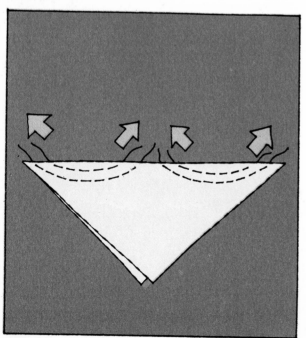

Fold the handkerchief in two and tack along the pencil marks with small stitches, then draw the threads tight to pucker up the material. You will then need to knot the threads together so that the cloth remains puckered throughout the dyeing operation. After removing the handkerchief from the dye, rinse it and then iron it while it is still damp.

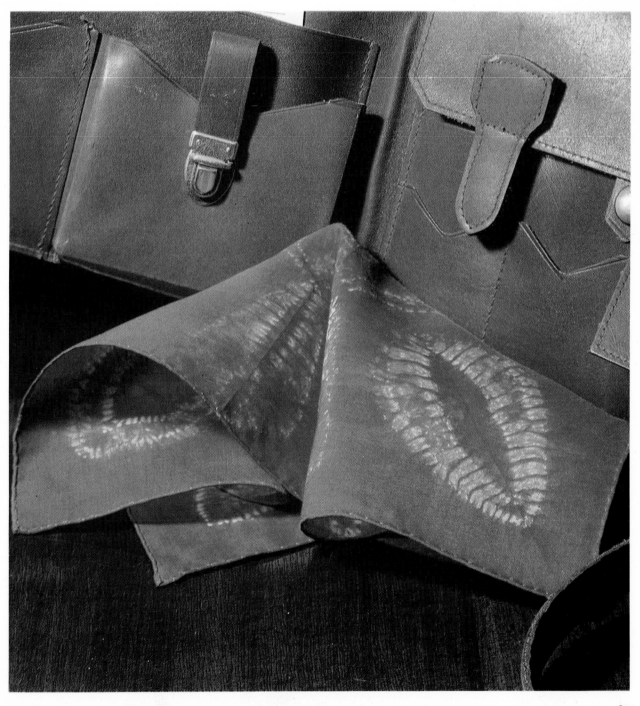

HEADSCARF

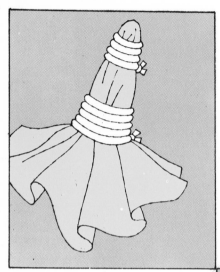

Tie the cloth as shown in the drawings. Use three baths of dye in the following order: yellow, blue, and red.

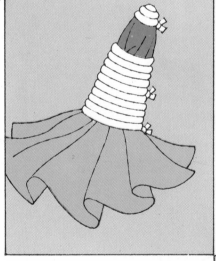

The cloth is tied at a different place each time so as to produce the alternating colors shown in the drawing on the next page.

Remember to rinse the scarf in cold water after each dyeing operation. You can draw out a few threads on each of the short sides to make a fringe about 1 in. long.

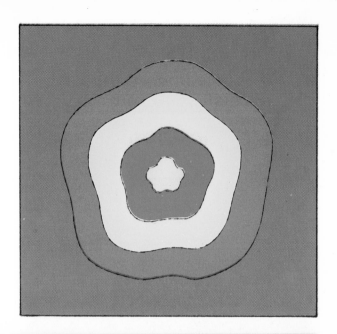

MATERIALS:
- White linen tablecloth
- Thick white cotton thread
- Green and purple dyes

TABLECLOTH

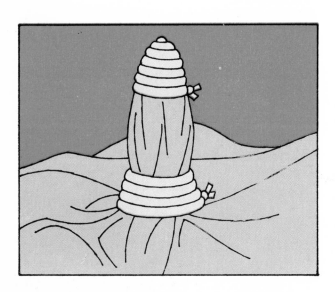 

Tie the cloth as shown, making sure that the knots are evenly spaced over the whole of the cloth surface. The threads used for tying should be arranged so as to produce concentric circles on the edge and at the center of each pattern (see page 87), with radiating stripes between them (see page 88). It is important to make sure that you use a really good quality dye for this job, since a tablecloth has to be washed frequently and if the dyes run or fade, the whole piece of work will be rapidly spoiled.

When preparing the dye, remember that a tablecloth is large and made of fairly thick material. Make sure that you have enough for the cloth to be properly soaked in the liquid. Read the manufacturer's instructions on the quantity of dye needed for the weight of material.

The dyeing is done in the following order: first purple, then green. After the first dyeing, keep the areas you want white bound with cotton. Bind the areas you want to remain purple with more cotton. Rinse, then dye the cloth with the second color.

HANDKERCHIEF

With this piece of work, we start using the batik method of dyeing.
Pin the cloth to a wooden frame or board and draw the letters and border design with a brush dipped in the molten wax. Make sure that you drain any excess wax from the brush on the side of the container each time that you dip it, since too much wax on the cloth will result in a blurred outline.

When the design is completed, dip the handkerchief in cold water and then in the bath of dye. Do not wring. The cold water will cause the wax to crack slightly, and this allows the dye to stain narrow streaks of the fabric; this gives the characteristic quality of batik.
When the dye has soaked well into the unwaxed parts of the material, take it out of the bath and hang it up to dry. It is a good idea to spread newspapers on the floor to catch any drips of dye.

When the material is dry, the wax can be removed with blotting paper and a hot iron (see page 89).

MATERIALS:

- Piece of white cotton batiste 18×15 in.
- Hot wax (see page 88)
- Dye
- Brush
- Blotting paper
- Iron

TRAY CLOTH

Pin the cloth to a board or frame and paint on the design as shown.
To give some variation to the design, paint some of the flower petals with only a very little wax on the brush. This means that the cloth will not be completely impregnated with wax and will absorb some of the dye.

When the design is completed, remove the material from the board, dip it in cold water, and then put it into the bath of dye.

As soon as the material has taken on the desired color, remove it from the dye, rinse, and leave to dry. Then place it between two sheets of blotting paper and iron with a hot iron to remove the wax from the material.

The tray cloth should be neatly hemmed on all four sides with cotton.

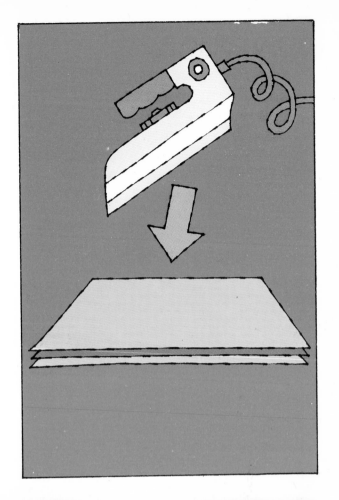

PIRATE FLAG

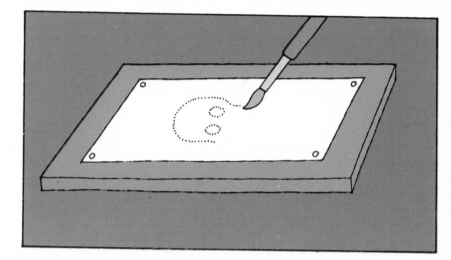

Fix the white cloth to your working frame or board and paint on a skull and cross bones with the brush dipped in wax. Remember to dab the brush against the edge of the container to remove any excess liquid. If the wax drips or runs on the design you will be left with white spots or a blurred outline after dyeing.

When the design is complete, dip the cloth in cold water and then black dye. The container for this should be deep enough for the cloth to be completely submerged in the dye without folding.

When the uncovered part of the cloth has thoroughly absorbed the color, remove the cloth from the dye and leave it to dry. Place some newspaper or a container underneath it while it is drying to catch the drops of black dye which will run off it.

When the material is completely dry, iron it between two sheets of blotting paper to remove the wax.

Cut the dyed material and the black piece of cloth to the shape shown in the drawing and sew them together around the edges to form the flag.

At the top, insert a wooden stick or a thick piece of cardboard between the two pieces of material. A piece of string can be attached to the ends of the stick so that the flag can be hung up.

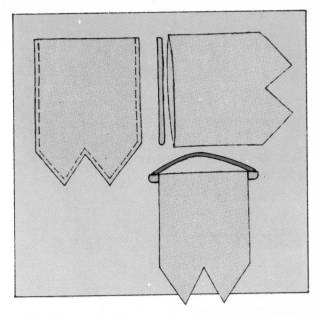

MATERIALS:

- Piece of white cloth 25×15 in.
- Dye
- Hot wax (see page 88)
- Blotting paper
- Iron
- Brush

ARMBAND

This is another piece of batik work. The dyeing is carried out as indicated on the preceding pages—102, 104, and 106.

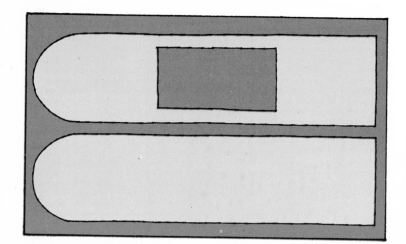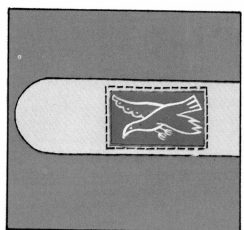

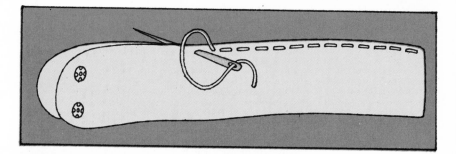

When the cloth is dry, sew it onto the armband made of white material; the band is made double, as shown in the drawing, to give it more strength.

The armband is fastened around the arm with tapes or press studs.

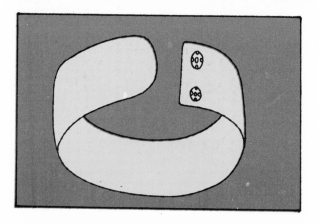

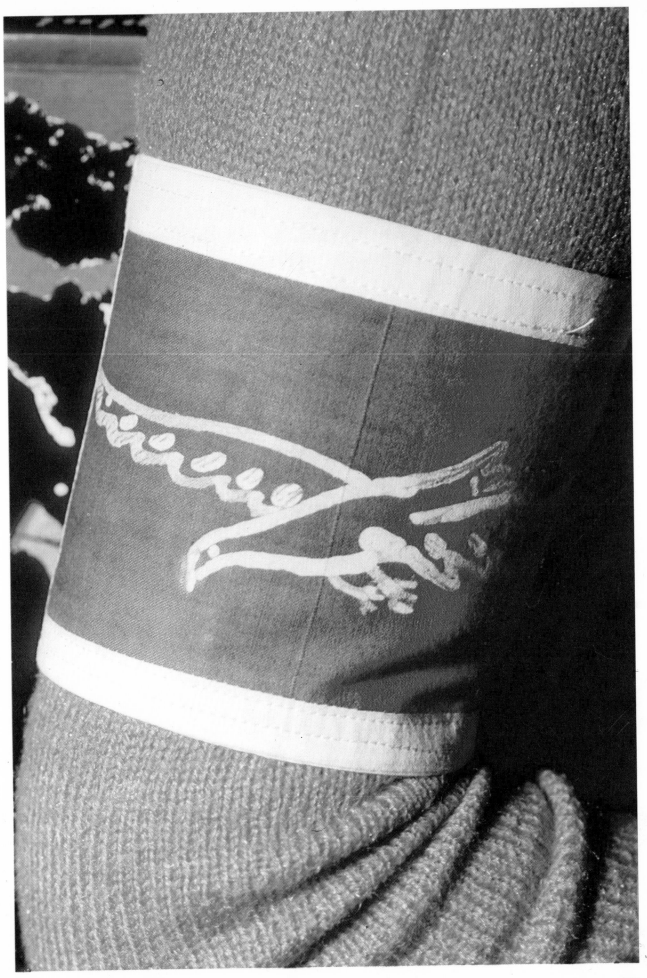

MATERIALS:
- Piece of interlining felt 25×15 in.
- Hot wax (see page 88)
- Dye
- Blotting paper
- Iron
- Brush

PENNANT

Fasten the felt to the frame or board. With the brush dipped in the hot wax, paint on the name and the design you wish. If you want to draw the design first in pencil on the material, use a soft pencil and press very lightly.

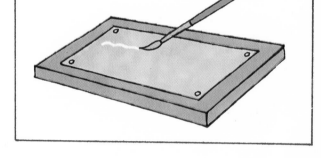

When the design is complete and the felt well impregnated with wax, dip it in the bath of dye. As soon as the felt has taken on the desired color, remove it from the liquid, rinse and leave it to dry; remember to put some newspaper or an old cloth underneath to catch the drips.

When the work is dry, it can be ironed between two sheets of blotting paper to remove the wax.
Finally, cut it to the shape usual for this type of pennant.

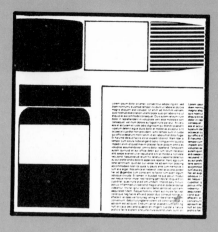

Working with paper mâché

The French term "papier mâché," which means pulped paper, describes an artistic technique which uses paper soaked in water and glue.

The technique is said to have been used by the Chinese in ancient times for making the giant dragons which appeared in festivals and parades.

Since then, the ways of working with pulped paper have gone through many changes and variations.

In this book, we use three different ways of working with wet paper and glue. In each case we use newspaper, as it is the most absorbent.

The adhesive used is either a paste made from PVA glue or a cellulose wallpaper paste. The adhesive is mixed with the water until it thickens, so that when one dips one's fingers in the mixture they stick together and it requires a little effort to separate them.

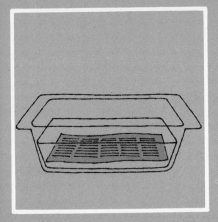

The three ways of working with papier mâché are as follows:

1. The newspaper is soaked in the mixture of glue and water; then it is folded into the desired shape. There are various examples in the book which use this method.

2. The newspaper is cut into very small pieces and left soaking in water for several hours; then it is taken out and squeezed to remove excess liquid.

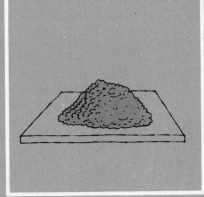

The pulp is then mixed with PVA glue or cellulose paste and placed on a board. The resulting mixture is rather sticky, but can be easily worked if it is kneaded for a while beforehand.

If a very fine pulp is required, the soaked paper and adhesive can be put in an electric blender. The resulting paste can be used for modeling figures as if it were clay or plasticine. It has the advantage of being much cheaper and of going fairly hard when it dries. It can also be decorated very easily with paint, if this is prepared in the right way.

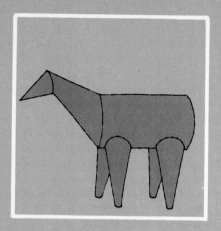

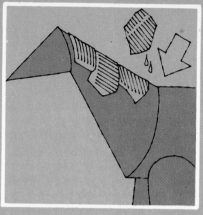

3. A framework of cardboard, wire or wood is made first as a basis for the figure. This is then covered with small pieces of newspaper soaked in paste. When the whole of the figure has been covered in this way, it is left to dry until all the moisture has evaporated.

Finally a coating of paper pulp is applied, prepared in the way described previously. The features of the figure are then molded.

The figure should be allowed to dry naturally. If you try to accelerate the process by placing it near a radiator or other source of heat, there is a risk of the paper cracking or becoming distorted.

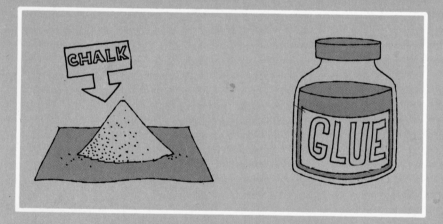

When the paper is completely dry, it can be given a coating of powdered chalk mixed with carpenter's glue. This mixture should be applied while warm, and should be of a fairly thick consistency so that it covers the surface properly.

When the layer of chalk and glue is completely dry, any irregularities may be removed with sandpaper. Take care not to scratch the surface too much and not to dent the figure. Being hollow it is not very resistant to pressure.

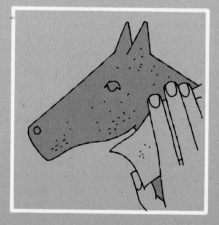

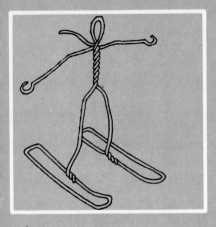

If a very smooth surface is required, give the figure several coats of chalk and glue, sand-papering between each one.

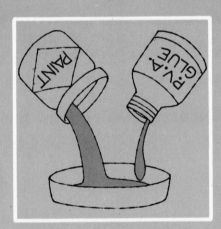

Painting the objects will make them look even better. Tempera or gouache should be used.

A small amount of PVA glue should be mixed with these paints just before using them, to make the paper figures more waterproof.

Since gouache dries with a matt effect, the PVA glue is also essential if the finished object is to have a shiny surface like glazed china. For this purpose you should not only mix glue with the paint, but the object should also be given a final coating of PVA.

NAPKIN RINGS

Cut the newspaper into pieces approximately 16×9 in. Each of these pieces will make a ring. Cover the whole of one side of the piece of newspaper with glue and then fold it over and over to form a strip about 2 in. wide and 9 in. long.

Join the two ends of this strip to make the ring. When the glue is quite dry, cover the ring with a coating of paper pulp and leave it to dry.

Paint the rings whatever color you wish, and when the paint is dry they can be decorated by sticking on pictures or photographs cut out of magazines. These decorations should then be covered with a coat of plastic varnish. This must be applied with a very soft brush so that it does not remove the first layer of paint, which could go patchy or mark the decorations.

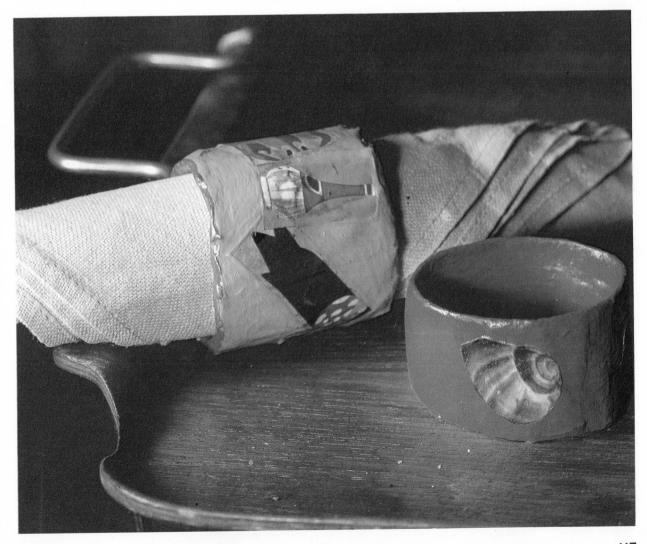

CANDLESTICKS

Make three similar rings from newspaper (see page 116). Cover them with paper pulp and stick them together as shown in the drawing, to form the base of the candlestick, reinforcing the joint with strips of paper.

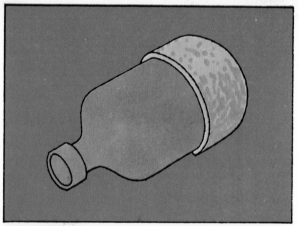

Make the candle holder by rolling strips of paper around the end of a bottle, and then fastening it to the top of the base.

Stick a large pin through the bottom of the holder, point upward, to take the candle.

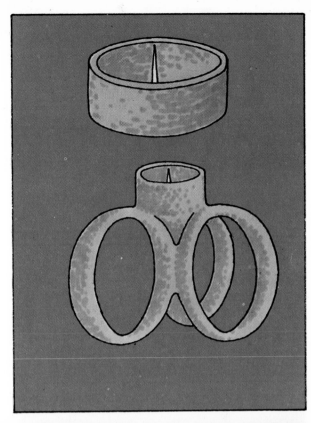

When all the parts of the candlestick
are completely dry it can be painted.
A little PVA glue should be added to
the paint to give it a glossy finish and
make the surface of the candlestick
waterproof.

As with all candles, be very careful
when you light them, in case of
accident. Never leave a candle burn-
ing if you are out of the room.

MATERIALS:
- Cardboard, PVA glue
- Paper pulp (see page 113)
- Paints (see page 115)
- Piece of plastic sheet

FLOWERPOT HOLDER

Cut the sides and base of the holder out of cardboard.

Stick the two ends of the rectangle together to form a wide tube. The round piece of cardboard forming the base is then stuck to one end of this tube.

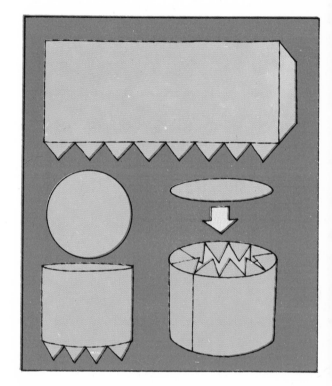

Reinforce the join between these two pieces with a strip of newspaper stuck around the edge.

When the glue is quite dry, cover the whole container with a thin layer of paper pulp. Leave this to dry, then line the container with plastic sheeting as shown in the drawing. The top edge of the plastic is held in place by a second layer of paper pulp.

When the holder is quite dry, it can be painted. You should mix plenty of PVA glue with the paint so that the colors come out very glossy and the holder is practically waterproof and well protected against any moisture which may seep from the flowerpot inside.

121

BOWL

Cover the outside of the bowl with a layer of paper pulp $\frac{1}{4}$ in. thick, pressing it well down so that it sticks to the surface of the bowl and takes its shape perfectly.

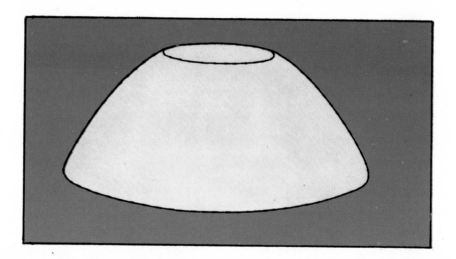

Leave it to dry away from direct heat; it is important not to place it near a radiator or, if it is summer, in the sun, as it may crack.

When the papier mâché bowl is completely dry, it can be separated from the mold and painted, then given a coat of PVA glue.

BOX

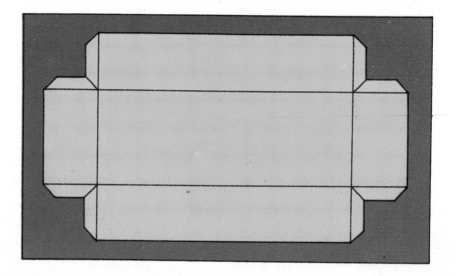

Cut two pieces of cardboard to the pattern shown in the drawings on this page. Then stick them to make the box and lid. When the glue is dry, cover both parts of the box with a thin layer of papier mâché.

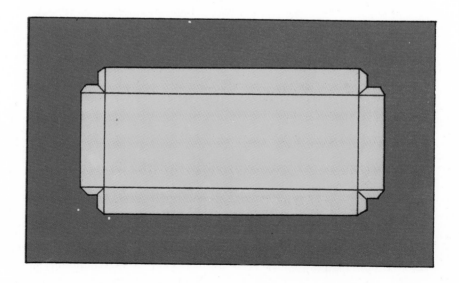

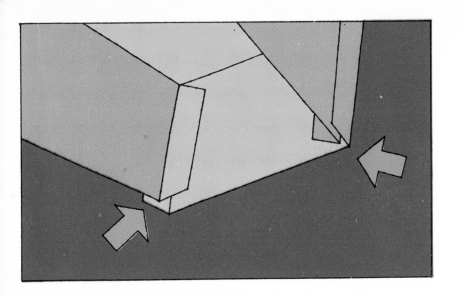

After a few hours, when the paper is completely dry, you can begin to decorate the box with specially prepared paints.
Wait for one coat of paint to dry before applying anotner over the top, otherwise the colors may run.

MATERIALS:

- Paper pulp (see page 113)
- Cellophane in different colors
- Paints (see page 115), PVA glue
- Wooden sticks $\frac{1}{4}$ in. square
- Large, brass-headed carpet nail
- Two pieces of hard leather $\frac{3}{4} \times \frac{3}{4}$ in.

MODEL WINDMILL

Make the windmill (or houses, or trees) from well-kneaded papier mâché.
Paint and decorate each piece.

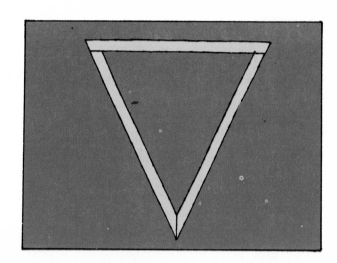

To make the sails of the windmill, first glue the wooden sticks into the shape shown in the drawing above. Then cover this framework with cellophane.

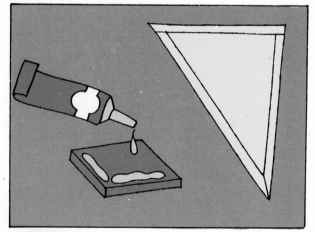

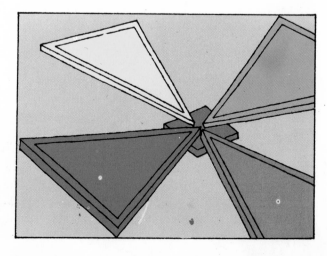

Finally, join the four sails together by sticking them on one of the pieces of leather, then reinforce the join by sticking the other piece on top.

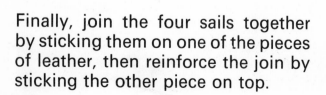

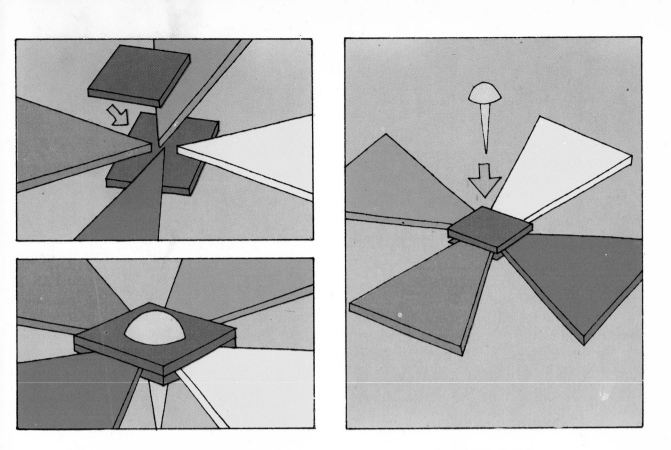

When the sails are finished, fix them in place with the carpet nail.

MASK

Model the face you want to give the mask in plasticine and then cover the whole surface with a thin coating of vaseline. This will prevent the paper soaked in glue from sticking to the mold.

Soak the pieces of newspaper thoroughly in the mixture of water and glue, then apply them to the plasticine mold, building up a layer about $\frac{1}{8}$ in. thick. Then leave the work to dry.

After six to eight hours the mask will be completely dry and can be separated easily from the mold.

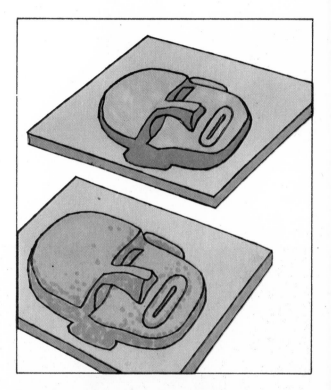

Decorate the mask with the paints. Make a small hole on either side at the top of the ear and insert a piece of elastic cord knotted at each end, to hold the mask on the head of the wearer. Stick strips of tissue paper to the forehead, and to the inside of the mask, so that they fall down on either side of the face.

PENCIL HOLDERS

Cut the rectangles and circles which will form the bases and sides of the holders out of cardboard.

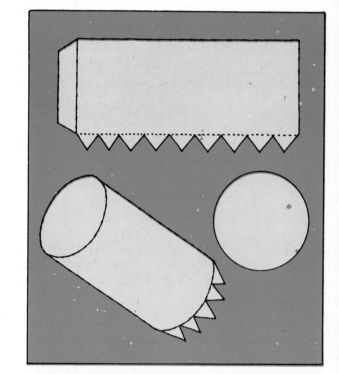

Join each rectangle end to end to form a tube, then attach the circle to the base as shown. The join can be reinforced by a strip of thin paper stuck around the edge.

Apply a thin layer of papier mâché to the cardboard and when this is completely dry, decorate each holder with paints. This decoration can also be done with cutouts from magazines, designs drawn on thin paper or paper transfers.

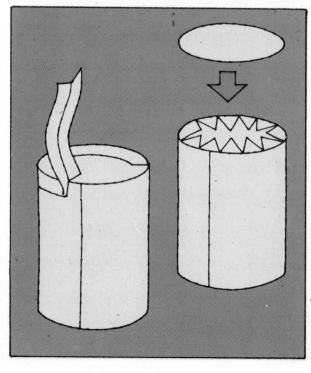

If the holders are decorated with paper cutouts, they must be covered with a thin coat of plastic varnish. This should be applied carefully after the first coat of paint has completely dried, so that the paint is not disturbed by the varnish.

BOOK ENDS

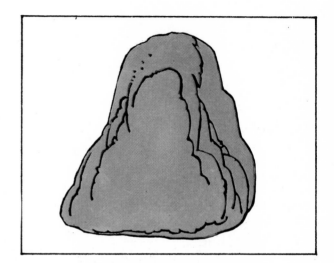

The stones serve as a basis for the groups of toadstools, giving them solidity and weight.

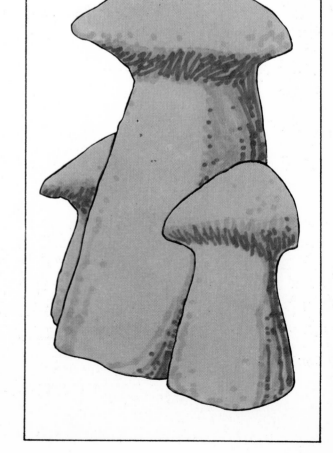

Apply a thick layer of papier mâché to the stones and model it into the shape of the toadstools. One of the sides of each group should be left completely flat, so that it can serve as a support for the books.

When the book end is completely dry it can be painted. The best method is to start from the top and work downwards, waiting for each color to dry before starting on another.

JAR TOPS

Cut out the circle first; it must be the right size to fit just inside the neck of the jar. Make the rectangle long enough to fit around the edge of the circle.

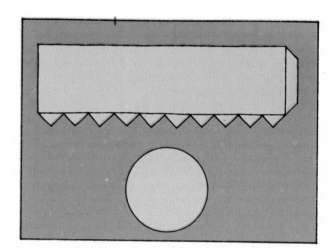

Join these two pieces to form a small round box; to do this, first join the two ends of the rectangle together and then stick the triangular tabs to the edges of the round piece. The join can be reinforced by a strip of thin paper stuck around the edge.

When the glue is quite dry, fill this box with paper pulp; press it well down, but take care not to distort the box, then leave it to dry.
Cut twelve pieces of newspaper to the shape shown on the right of the drawing; glue them on top of one another and leave them to dry.

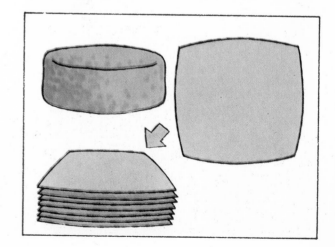

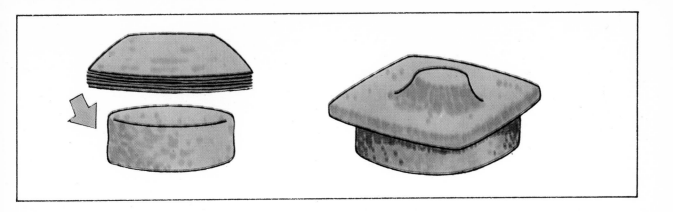

Form the knob from a small amount of papier mâché and stick it on top of the last piece. Then stick this on top of the round piece.
As soon as the lid is dry, it can be painted and decorated.

FLOWER VASE

Cut out two pieces of cardboard to the pattern shown in the drawing, to make two cones. These can be of whatever size you wish.

Cut the tips off the cones and stick them together, reinforcing the joint with a strip of cardboard which has cuts along both sides so that it can be bent into shape.

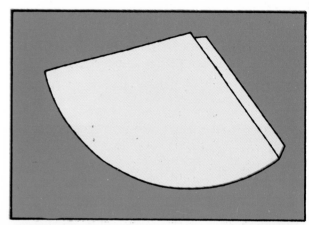

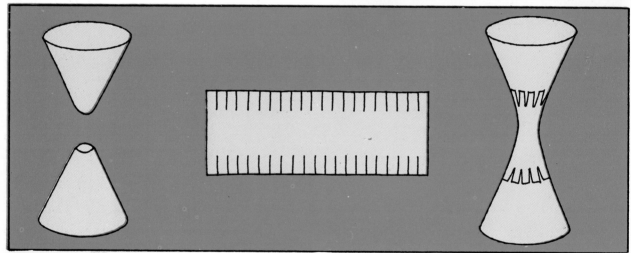

When the glue is dry, cover the whole vase with a thin layer of papier mâché. Leave to dry for four or five hours, then paint and decorate the vase, mixing a little PVA glue with the paint to bring out the colors and give a better surface.

Before putting in some dried flowers or branches, fill the vase with sand. This will weigh it down and give a better support for the contents.

This vase can only be used for dried flowers, as it will not be waterproof.

MATERIALS:

- Eight pieces of newspaper 15×5 in.
- Four pieces of newspaper 9×5 in.
- Three pieces of newspaper 30×5 in.
- PVA glue (see page 112)
- Paints (see page 115)

BASKET

Cover one side of each of the pieces of newspaper with glue and fold it over on itself lengthwise to make a strip approximately $\frac{3}{4}$ in. wide.

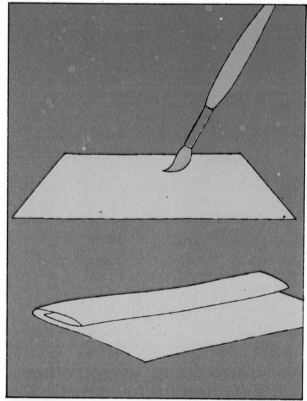

Interlace the eight 15 in. strips to make the bottom of the basket as shown in the drawing. Put a drop of glue at the point where each strip crosses another. This will make the bottom firmer, and the task of weaving the rest of the basket will be much easier.

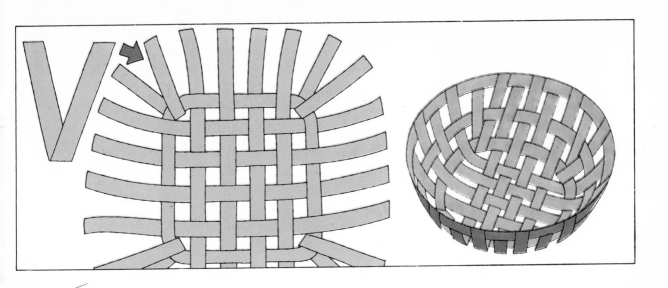

Weave one of the 30 in. strips around the outside of the base as shown, then fold each of the four 9 in. strips into a "V" and place them at the corners. Weave the remaining two 30 in. strips parallel to the first one and equally spaced, to form the sides of the basket. If any of the pieces come out too long, cut the extra piece off, then glue the end to the 30 in. strip.
Once the basket is finished and the glue completely dry, it can be painted in a single color or a combination of different colors.

MATERIALS:

- Piece of cardboard 8 × 4½ in.
- Copper or brass wire ⅛ in. thick
- Paper pulp (see page 113)
- Paints (see page 115)

BELT BUCKLE

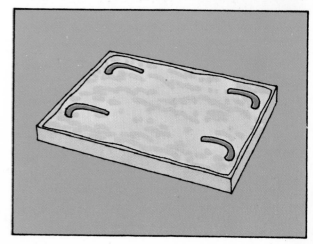

Fold the cardboard into a tray with sides ¼ in. high. Cover the bottom with a first layer of papier mâché, then place the pieces of wire on top of it with the ends bent over as shown. The length of the pieces of wire will depend on the total length you intend to make the buckle.

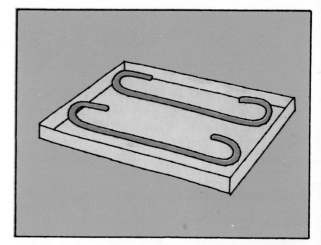

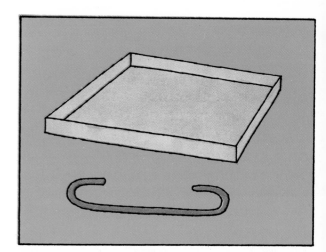

Cover the wires with another layer of papier mâché, completely filling the tray. It should then be left to dry over a source of heat such as a radiator.

When the buckle is completely dry, it can be decorated with tempera paints, which, when they are dry, should be covered with a coat of clear varnish.
The buckle is now ready to be mounted on the belt. The pieces of wire hook into the holes in the leather.

MATERIALS:

- Piece of white card 15×12½ in.
- PVA glue
- Paper pulp (see page 113)
- Paints (see page 115)
- Fine sandpaper

DOVE

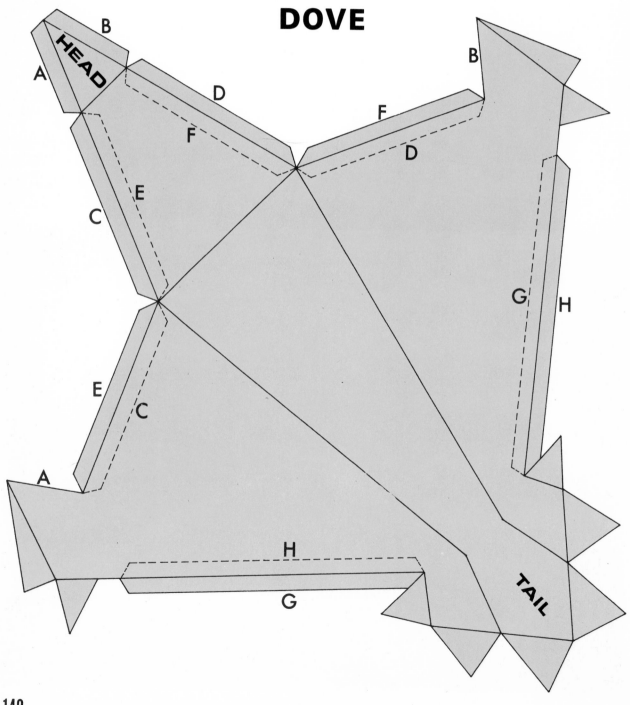

Draw the pattern shown in the drawing on the card, cut it out, and stick the tabs together as indicated by the letters: A to A, B to B, etc.

In places where double tabs are indicated, one of them should be stuck on the inside and the other on the outside; this will make the dove more solid and it will retain its shape better. When the card framework is completed and the glue is quite dry, cover the figure with a layer of papier mâché $\frac{1}{16}$ in. thick. Leave it to dry for 24 hours and then go over it carefully with fine sandpaper to remove any irregularities.

When the surface is completely smooth, it can be painted.

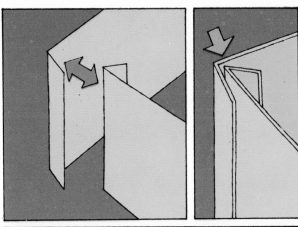

MATERIALS:

- Sheet of cardboard
- Four wooden sticks
- Paper pulp (see page 113)
- Paints (see page 115)

HORSE

Make a cylinder of card and stick it firmly all along its length.

When the glue is dry, make four holes in the cylinder and insert the sticks which form the basis of the legs. Put a drop of glue on the end of each stick so that it is attached to the inside of the cylinder, and also at the point where it passes through the holes in the cardboard.

When the sticks are firmly in place, make four cones of card to cover the legs; another larger cone is needed for the neck and a smaller one for the head.

These cones are then attached to the cylinder as shown in the drawing.

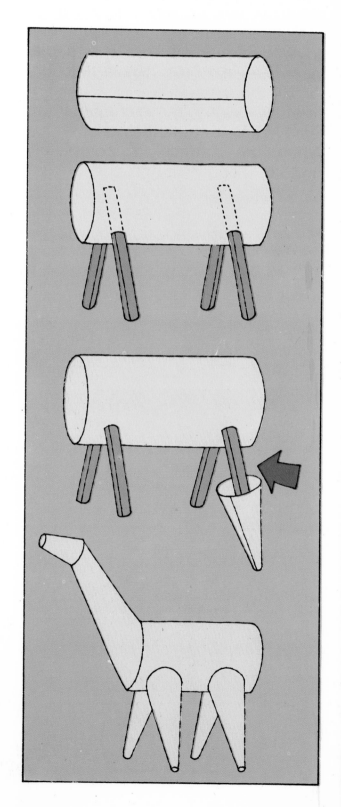

When fastening the cones to the body, stick a strip of paper around each joint to reinforce it.

The figure is then covered with a layer of newspaper pieces ($\frac{1}{16}$ in. thick) soaked in a mixture of water and glue. When this is almost dry, apply a thin layer of paper pulp, modeling in the features of the horse: nose, ears, mane and tail.

If you wish to give it a very smooth surface, almost like china, apply a coat of powdered chalk and glue and leave it to dry. This final coat can be sandpapered gently to remove any roughness. Finally, paint the horse.

MATERIALS:
- Piece of wood 10 in. long and $2\frac{1}{2}$ in. wide
- Two large screws
- Paper pulp (see page 113)
- Paints (see page 115)

BOAT

Drive the two screws into one side of the piece of wood. These will serve as a basis for the funnels of the boat.

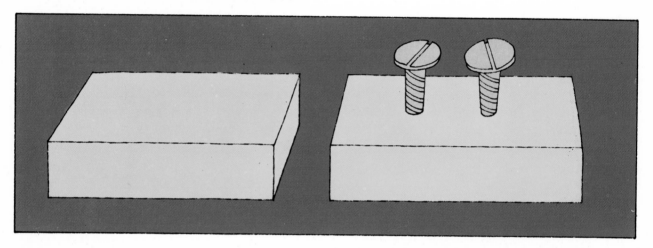

Build up successive layers of papier mâché around the wood until you have obtained the required shape and size.

As the papier mâché will probably be very thick, you will need to leave the boat one or two days to dry.

When the boat is completely dry, it can be painted as shown in the photograph.

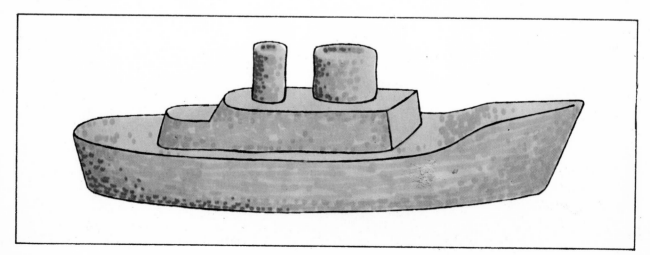

GLOVE PUPPETS

Blow up a balloon until it is the size required for the puppet's head. Cover the balloon with a thin layer of papier mâché, molding the features: nose, chin, curve of the eyebrow, ears.

Leave it to dry for about six hours, then let down the balloon and remove it through the neck.

Paint on the remaining features, and when the paint and PVA coating (if used) are quite dry, stick the woolen hair on top of the head.

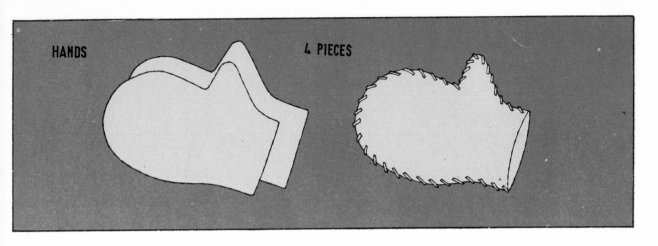

HANDS   4 PIECES

Each hand is made from two identical pieces, sewn together around the edge.

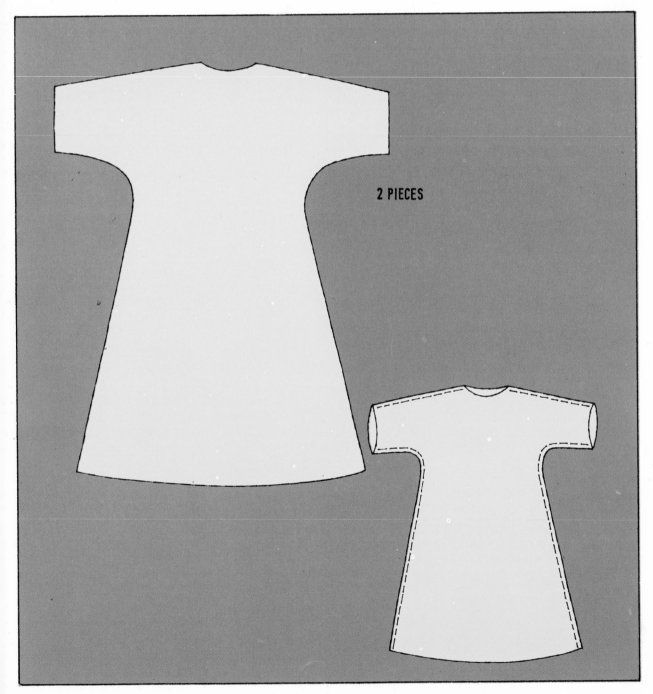

2 PIECES

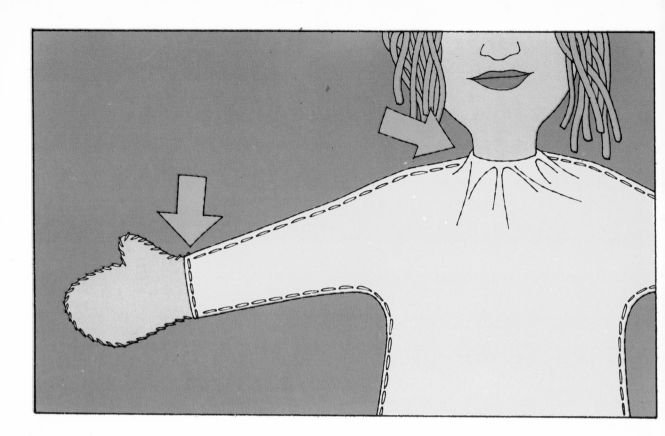

The hands are then sewn to the sleeves of the puppet's clothing. This is stuck to the base of the head and the join is covered by a piece of morocco decorated with beads, which forms a collar.

The belt is made from a strip of morocco, fringed at each end and fastened by a small strip of metal which acts as a clasp. It is fastened to the clothing by a couple of stitches at the sides.

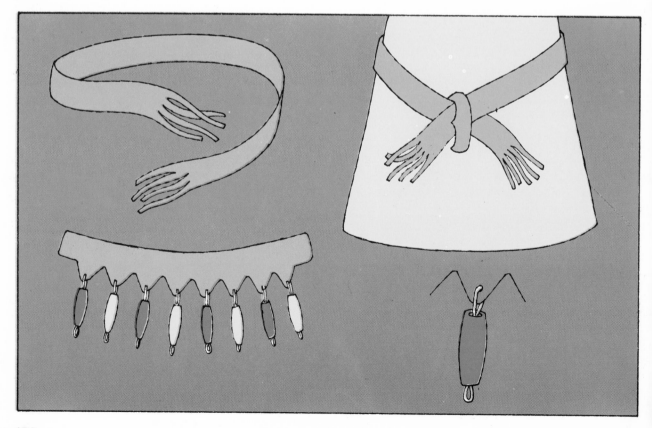

PEACOCK

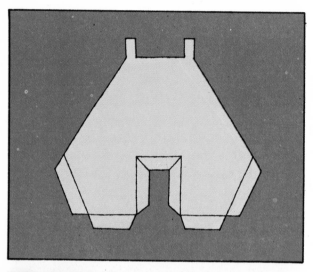

Cut the various pieces shown in the drawings out of cardboard. Two identical pieces are needed for the tail. They are joined together by tabs at the top.

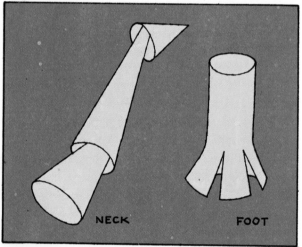

NECK   FOOT

The head, neck and body of the peacock are made from different sized cones, which are inserted into one another and then glued.
The feet are made from two cylinders, with cuts made in the end to form the claws. These must be large and solid as they form the main support for the figure, which would otherwise tend to overbalance when filled with pencils.

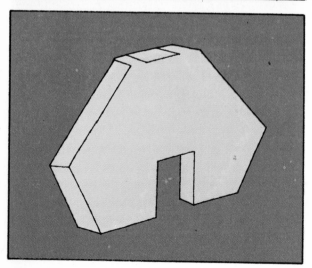

When all the pieces have been made, stick them together and cover them with a thin layer of papier mâché. After four or five hours, the work can be painted. Mix a small amount of PVA glue with the paints to give a gloss to the colors and a better surface to the whole figure.

MATERIALS:

- Paper pulp (see page 113)
- Two metal washers (not essential)
- Sisal string
- Dried flower
- Two nails sharpened at both ends
- PVA glue and paints

CLOWN

Make the various parts of the doll out of solid papier mâché. When they are completely dry—which will take about 24 hours—join the head to the body and body to feet with the double ended nails. Before sticking these in, apply some glue to the area where the two parts will meet, to strengthen the join. The two washers, if inserted at the neck and ankles, will also help to give greater strength at these points.

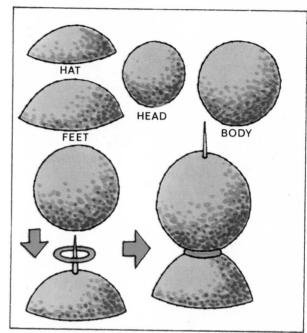

When these joints are dry, the doll can be painted. It is best to start from the top and work downward. The hat is best painted before being attached to the head.

Make the hair from several short pieces of sisal string knotted at one end. Unravel the ends and stick the hair to the top of the clown's head. When the glue fixing the hair has dried, the hat can be stuck on top of it.

Finally, stick a dried flower between the strands of hair.

TUMBLER TOY

To make the bottom part of the doll, prepare the papier mâché and line the inside of a bowl with it. When you have built up the lining to about $\frac{1}{2}$ in. thick, place the lead weights in the center, then continue to fill the bowl until the papier mâché is level with the top. Leave it to dry, and then remove it from the bowl.

Meanwhile you can prepare the upper part, which is made from a cone of cardboard. Stick this cone to the bottom part as soon as the papier mâché is completely dry.

Next, cover the whole surface of the figure with papier mâché, modeling in the main features of the face, and the arms and tray. The bottle is modeled separately in papier mâché and then stuck to the tray with a drop of PVA glue.

When the papier mâché is completely dry, the figure can be decorated with paints mixed with a small amount of PVA glue.

TRAY

Cut about 20 sheets of newspaper to the size required for the tray. Soak them in the glue and water mixture and place them one on top of the other. Cover them with the plastic sheet to protect the books which should now be placed on top to keep the paper flat while it dries. This will take some time—24 hours or more—since the major part of the surface is covered by the plastic.

It is a good idea to raise the plastic away from the paper around the edges so that the water can seep out more easily.

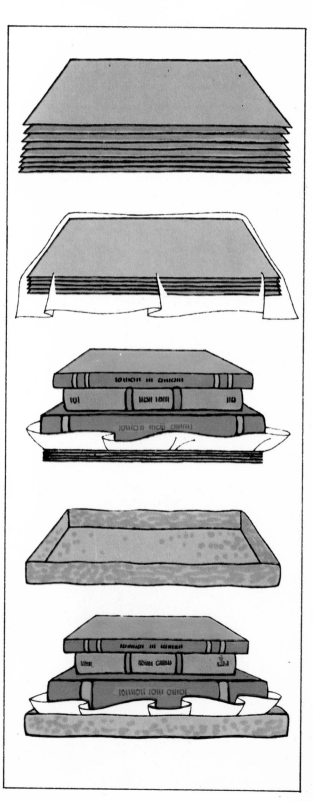

When the base is quite dry, build up the sides with papier mâché and leave this to dry once more for several hours. Do not remove the books from the center of the tray, since the water from the edges could otherwise distort the bottom.

As soon as the papier mâché has completely dried out, the tray can be painted and decorated. The amount of glue added to the paint should be quite substantial in this case, to bring out the colors and make the tray more or less waterproof.

MATERIALS:
● Cardboard
● Paper pulp (see page 113)
● Paints (see page 115)

BUTTERFLIES

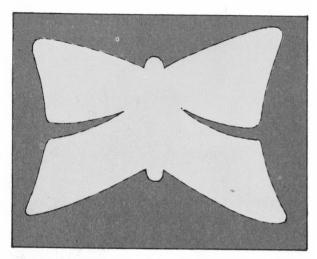

Cut the silhouettes of the butterflies out of the cardboard. Each butterfly can be a different size, with slightly different proportions between the wings and the body.

Cover the cardboard with papier mâché, building up the body in the center and scoring the pattern of the markings on the wings. The marks will accentuate the different colors when the butterflies are painted.

When papier mâché is applied to only one side of the cardboard, it usually warps with the dampness. It is better not to try to flatten it again, and in any case a slight curve will make the butterfly look more realistic.

When the papier mâché is completely dry it can be painted. If some of the colors are mixed with PVA glue and others not, the contrast of matt and glossy colors will make the markings on the wings look more attractive.

MATERIALS:
● Two cardboard boxes
● PVA glue, paints
● Paper pulp (see page 113)
● Three pieces of wire
● Newspaper and glue
   mixture

SMALL SHELF

Cut the two cardboard boxes into the shapes shown
in the drawing, then stick them end to end. When
the glue is dry, start covering the boxes with pieces
of newspaper soaked in glue and water (see page
114).
Cover this first layer of glued paper with a second
coating of paper pulp.

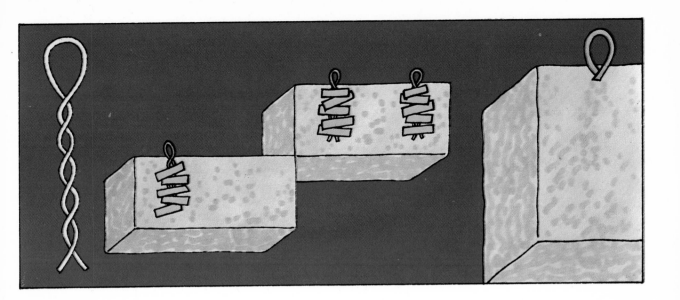

Make three loops of wire as shown in the drawing. The shank should be long enough to reach almost to the bottom of the shelf.

Fasten the loops to the back of the shelving as shown and cover them well with strips of gummed paper, then later with papier mâché, so that they are well buried and there is no danger of their coming out when weight is placed on the shelves.

Leave the work to dry thoroughly and then paint it as desired.

COAT RACK

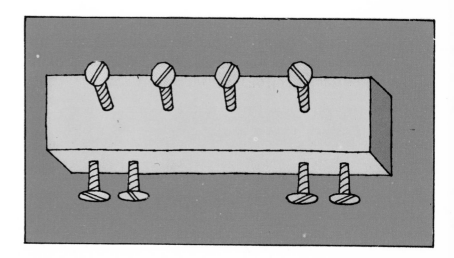

Screw the eight screws into the wood to form a base on which to build up the dog's legs and the pegs. This will make them strong and able to take the weight of coats.

Screw the eyes into the top of the wood.

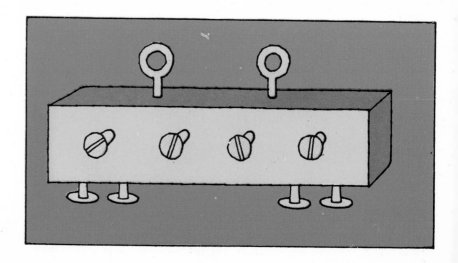

Cover the wood with a thick layer of papier mâché, modeling it into the shape of the dog. It is a good idea to do this on some sheets of dry newspaper, so that you can move the dog without disturbing the shape; at the same time the back can be kept completely flat, as it will need to be for the rack to hang properly against the wall.

As this job uses a lot of papier mâché, it will take a long time to dry. You will need to leave it for four or five days before starting to paint it.

PICTURE FRAME

Draw the outline of the glass on the wood with a pencil. Put some PVA glue on this outer area which is to form the frame and cover it with papier mâché. Make sure that the frame is of an even width all the way around; the papier mâché should be about ½ in. deep.

When the frame is finished, and before the papier mâché has dried, try the glass in the space left for it to make sure that it fits properly; press the papier mâché in around the glass to remove any irregularities.

Then lift the glass out with the help of a needle or spike and fill in the groove which this will have left. If the glass has been smeared by the wet papier mâché, wash the marks off before they dry.

When the frame is dry it can be given a first coat of blue paint. Two coats will be needed so that both the background and the frame take the color properly. Mix some resin PVA glue with the paint (see page 115) to bring out the colors.

When the blue paint is dry, paint the stripes on the frame. When these have dried, stick the dried flowers to the background, then place the glass in position, apply PVA glue all the way around where it meets the frame, and fix the piece of cord on top of the join. Another piece of cord should be attached to the back of the frame so that it can be hung from the wall.

MATERIALS:

- **White cardboard**
- **Newspaper**
- **Paper pulp (see page 113)**
- **PVA glue**
- **26 pieces of white string each 15 in. long**
- **54 wooden beads**
- **Paints (see page 115)**

LAMP SHADE

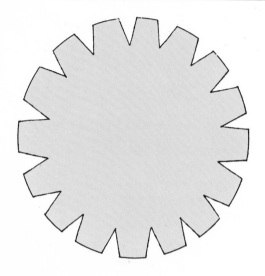

Cut a round piece of cardboard 15 in. in diameter. Then cut tabs around the edges as shown in the drawing.

Place the piece of cardboard in the bottom of a round tray or dish the same size as that required for the lamp shade. The tags around the edge should be well impregnated with glue and bent upward, overlapping where necessary so that they are an exact fit inside the container being used as a mold.

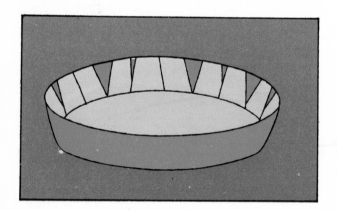

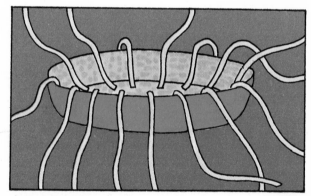

Cover the cardboard with a layer of papier mâché and before this is completely dry arrange the pieces of string on top of it as shown in the drawing. Then apply another layer of papier mâché so as to cover the ends of the string and hold them in place.

168

While this layer of papier mâché is drying, you can prepare the rings and tubes which will form the fringes of the lamp shade. These pieces are made by the method shown on page 116 for making napkin rings.

When the main body of the lamp shade is dry, remove it from the mold and cut a hole 2½ in. in diameter in the centre.

Make a cylinder of cardboard the same size as the hole, and fix it in place as shown, reinforcing the joint with a strip of paper soaked in glue and water mixture.

Then cover the whole of the top of the lamp shade with papier mâché.

As soon as all the parts are dry they can be painted.

The beads, rings and tubes are threaded onto the pieces of string to make the fringe of the lamp shade. Tie a knot in the end of each string to prevent the decorations from falling off.

SKIER

With the help of the pliers, make a wire skeleton (as shown below) which will serve as a foundation for the papier mâché figure.

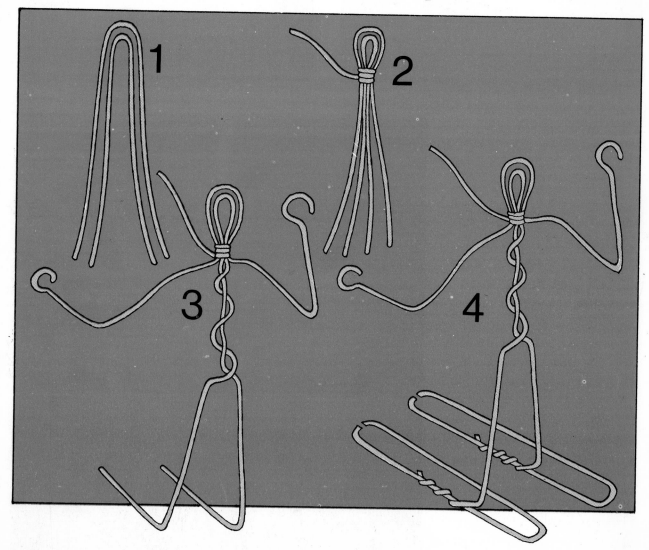

The skeleton should first be covered with pieces of newspaper soaked in glue and water mixture (see page 115). When you have built up the body to almost the required thickness, apply a final layer of paper pulp, modeling in the main features of the figure. When this final layer of papier mâché is dry, the figure can be painted; add a little PVA glue to the paint to bring out the colors.

MATERIALS:
- ● **Paper pulp (see page 113)**
- ● **Balloon**
- ● **Paints (see page 115)**
- ● **Wool for the hair**
- ● **Materials for the body and clothes**
- ● **Kapok for stuffing the body**

DOLL'S HEAD AND HANDS

The head of the doll is made in exactly the same way as that of the glove puppets on page 148. For the hands, begin by making a silhouette out of papier mâché, then mark the fingers on it with a toothpick and hollow out the palm. When making the hands, two things should be borne in mind: they should be in proportion with the head, and one should be a left hand, one a right hand.

When the head and hands are dry, they can be painted. The amount of PVA glue added to the paint can be varied, so that by combining matt and gloss colors you can get a better "make-up" effect on the face.

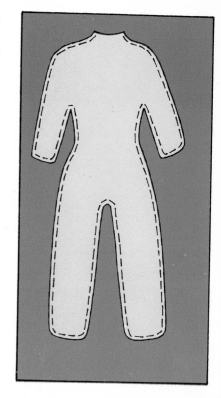

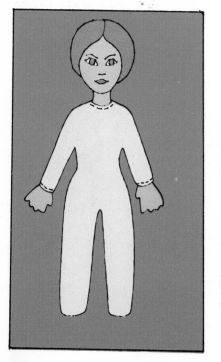

The body is made by sewing together two pieces of material along the dotted line shown in the drawing. It is then filled with kapok and the head and hands are attached by being stitched to the neck and the ends of the arms with strong thread. The doll shown here is only one example of the many types which are possible. The face and clothing can be made to represent any type of historical or fictional character, and you can, for instance, make a collection of kings and queens, or storybook heroes.

MATERIALS:
- **Paper pulp (see page 113)**
- **Eight foolscap sheets of strong paper**
- **PVA glue**
- **Paints (see page 115)**

NATIVITY FIGURES

All the human figures, including that of the child, are begun with a sheet of paper rolled into a cone and trimmed off at the top and bottom.

Place a ball of papier mâché on top of the cone to form the head of the figure. Using a needle or toothpick, mark the features of the face while the paper is still wet.

Cover the cone with papier mâché, modeling in the arms and other raised parts of the body.

When the figure is finished, it should be left to dry for at least 24 hours before being painted.

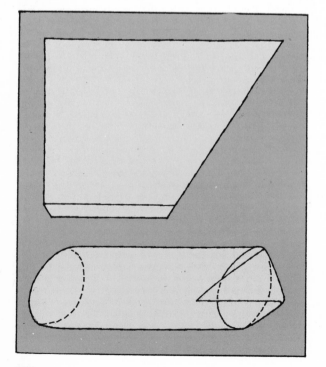

The two animals, the mule and the ox, are based on a piece of paper cut as shown in the drawing, then rolled up to make a rounded, oblong shape with a sloping snout at one end. This is then covered with papier mâché which is modelled to form the features (ears, nose, etc.) of the animals.

The child's cradle is based on a paper box constructed as shown in the drawing. This is then covered with a layer of papier mâché about $\frac{1}{8}$ in. thick.

When all the figures are quite dry, paint them with gouache or tempera, adding a little PVA glue to bring out the colors and give the figures a slightly glazed appearance.

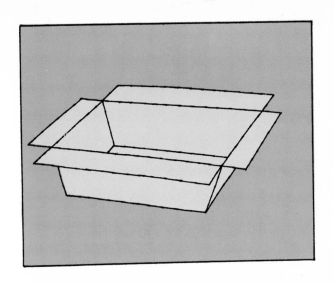

INDEX

3